The Fans Have Their Say #15 My Chemical Romance

Ian Carroll is a best selling author, with all of paperback and also on Kindle.

Ian is the author of the 'A-Z of Bloody Horror' bo *'Warning: Water May Contain Mermaids', 'Ant 'Pensioner'.* Also the author of the horror book *Pirates Vs. Vikings – Blackhorn's Revenge', Dating', 'Valentines Day'* and the joint horror Book *'Phantoms'* with Paddy Mullen.

'Hammer Horror' is also the first book in *'The Movie Fans Have Their Say'* series of Books, with many more planned for the future.

He is also the author of the music books –
'Lemmy: Memories of a Rock 'N' Roll Legend' – which was a #1 in the UK, USA, Canada, France and Germany – *'Ronnie James Dio: Man on the Silver Mountain – Memories of a Rock 'N' Roll Icon', 'Leonard Cohen: Just One More Hallelujah', 'Music, Mud and Mayhem: The Official History of the Reading Festival'* and *'From Donington to Download: The History of Rock at Donington Park'*.

The First Fourteen Volumes of the *'Fans Have Their Say…'* series are also available which are:

'The Fans Have Their Say #1   KISS - We Wanted the Best and We Got the Best'.
'The Fans Have Their Say #2   AC/DC – Rock 'N' Roll From the Land Down Under'.
'The Fans Have Their Say #3   BLACK SABBATH – The Lords of Darkness'.
'The Fans Have Their Say #4   GUNS 'N ROSES – Welcome to the Jungle…'
'The Fans Have Their Say #5   METALLICA – Exit, Light, Enter, Night'
'The Fans Have Their Say #6   QUEEN – Is This the Real Life…?'
'The Fans Have Their Say #7   ELTON JOHN – Count the Headlights on the Highway…'
'The Fans Have Their Say #8   MEAT LOAF – All Revved Up…'
'The Fans Have Their Say #9   DEF LEPPARD – Steel-City Rock Stars'
'The Fans Have Their Say #10 BON JOVI – New Jersey's Finest'
'The Fans Have Their Say #11 CINDERELLA – A Rock 'N' Roll Fairytale'
'The Fans Have Their Say #12 MOTLEY CRUE - L.A. Rock 'n' Roll Bad Boys'
'The Fans Have Their Say #13 WHITESNAKE – In the Still of the Night'
'The Fans Have Their Say #14 JOAN JETT – Punk's Not Dead!!!'

Ian has also written the history section for the Official Reading Festival music site in the UK and has attended the festival 33 times since 1983.

Ian lives with his wife Raine, two sons – Nathan & Josh - plus Stanley and the memories of a jet-black witches cat called Rex - in Plymouth, Devon, UK.

Facebook.com/iancarrollauthor (Various Book Pages as well)
iancarrollauthor@me.com

The Fans Have Their Say #15 My Chemical Romance

© Ian Carroll 2022

ISBN – 9798837171635

No part of this publication can be reproduced in any form or by any means, electronic or mechanical – including photocopy, recording or via any other retrieval system, without written permission from the Author/Publishers.

All other Photographs/Posters and covers of My Chemical Romance's LP's remain the copyright of the various associated production and distribution companies and are presented here for educative and review purposes only (under 'Fair Use' rules) to spread the knowledge and adoration of this artist and should not be reproduced in any way.

The Fans Have Their Say #15

My Chemical Romance

You Say EMO Like It's A Bad Thing?

© Ian Carroll 2022

The Fans Have Their Say #15 My Chemical Romance

The Fans Have Their Say #15 My Chemical Romance

Introduction

I've been lucky enough to see My Chemical Romance seven in total.

I came across MCR for the first time when attending the Download Festival at Donington Park motor-racing track in the UK in June 2005. At the time I was starting to put together my book on the Monsters of Rock/Download Festivals and they were on the bill, in the tent on the Friday evening.

From this earlier show, I have gone on to see them headline both Download Festival and the Reading Festival in the UK, supporting Muse at Wembley stadium and the first date on the UK's **'The Black Parade'** tour at the Pavilions in my home town of Plymouth.

At each show I have been amazed at the adoration, overcoming adversity during the 'bottling' at Reading Festival and then returning five years later as the all conquering heroes to having the Muse fans in their hand at Wembley.

Like everyone else, I never expected them to reform. Having seen Frank (and interviewed him) in his various solo band guises and Gerard making **'The Umbrella Academy'** a huge Netflix success, it was the least expected reformation of recent years and then it was dashed by the arrival of the Coronavirus Pandemic. They had already sold out three stadium shows at the MK Dons football stadium in Milton Keynes and I had tickets for the Eden Sessions at the 'ecologically friendly' outdoor venue in Cornwall at St Austell – this was to be a 'warm-up' and has a capacity of only 6,000 and so is quite intimate.

But here we are again now, moving slowly through 2022, with a new normality in the distance on the horizon. The UK dates have all been rescheduled, with original tickets available for the newly arranged dates, so we all have something to look forward to once again.

Which then brings me to this book. The 15th in the series, covering all the bands that I like and have seen many times. The fans lead the book forward, telling their stories, their experiences and their album preferences and I collate them, add my own stories and thoughts and

The Fans Have Their Say #15 My Chemical Romance

bring together what I hope to be another successful and popular entry in the series. So, sit back, have a read, look at the photos and most of all –

'Killjoys, Make Some Noise…'

Ian Carroll (June 2022)

The Fans Have Their Say #15 My Chemical Romance

The Fans Have Their Say #15 My Chemical Romance

I Brought You My Bullets, You Brought Me Your Love

1) Romance……………………………………………………….1:02
2) Honey, This Mirror Isn't Big Enough for the Two of Us…..3:51
3) Vampires Will Never Hurt You……………..……………….5:26
4) Drowning Lessons………………………………………….…4:23
5) Our Lady of Sorrows………………………………………….2:05
6) Headfirst for Halos……………………………………………3:28
7) Skylines and Turnstiles………………………………………3:23
8) Early Sunsets Over Monroeville……………………………5:04
9) This Is the Best Days Ever…...………………………………2:12
10) Cubicles………………………………………………………3:51
11) Demolition Lovers……………………………………….…..6:06

Release Date: 23rd July 2002
Producer: Geoff Rickly
Singles: 'Vampires Will Never Hurt You', 'Honey This Mirror Isn't Big Enough for the Two of Us', 'Headfirst for Halos'

The Fans Have Their Say #15 My Chemical Romance

"It's extremely overrated for being derivative and not even very good."
Billy Thompson (Baton Rouge, Louisiana, USA)

Such an underrated album by them!!
Also 1 or 2 of the songs aren't on Spotify or Amazon music or iTunes and it sucks."
Eddie Palasch (USA)

"I think it needs a re-record.
I'm not saying it is a bad album, but I feel like it has the potential to live up to the same standards as the other albums and the quality of the recording is holding it back.
Overall, I do love this album and it has a very safe space in my cold black heart."
Jack Hughes (Newport, UK)

"Without this I think I would be dead."
Lilly Youngs (In the World)

"This album is honestly my favorite from the deep topics of 9/11 to the silence of Romance it hits hard.
But it also shows people it is ok to feel and that if you do feel it's not a bad thing.
It shows people it's ok to be yourself and you don't have to be scared. MCR definitely touched lives with the lyrics and caught people with their sound for their debut album."
Anastasia Milhomme (Jewett City, Connecticut, USA)

"I love that this album was written in someone's basement."
Cherise Lynn (Mishawaka, Indiana, USA)

"Honestly, not my fave.
Like I have to rank it #3 out there 5 albums. '**Black Parade…**' is my #1, then '**Revenge…**', '**Danger Days**' is #4 and lastly is '**Conventional Weapons**'."
Jeff Nolan (Parma Heights, Ohio, USA)

"'**Bullets…**' is my favorite MCR album.
It's raw, poetic and fierce. The energy in this album has a pure intensity that is very rare to feel while listening to an album.
The album opened my young 13-year-old eyes to coping with addiction and depression with beautifully haunting metaphors.

The Fans Have Their Say #15 My Chemical Romance

The album left such an impact on me that I got the figure off of the album art tattooed on my arm. The tattoo signifies the healing power of the album, and to embrace the shadow and light aspects of the self equally."
Jordan Merlino (Santa Fe, New Mexico, USA)

"ABSOLUTELY EPIC album; start to finish."
Andre Veach (USA)

"Wonderful album. Each song is so different from the other and that's what I love about this album."
Tafi Leigh Bryant (Tennessee, USA)

"It's not my favorite album, but it's not terrible."
Myranda Stan (Hamburg, New York, USA)

"Love this album."
Ritche Taala (Taguig, Philippines)

"Best album, can't change my mind."
Charles Hamel (USA)

The best album."
James Montgomery (Kernersville, North Carolina, USA)

"Bullets...' because it's their heaviest album."
Joselyn Arriaga (USA)

The Fans Have Their Say #15 My Chemical Romance

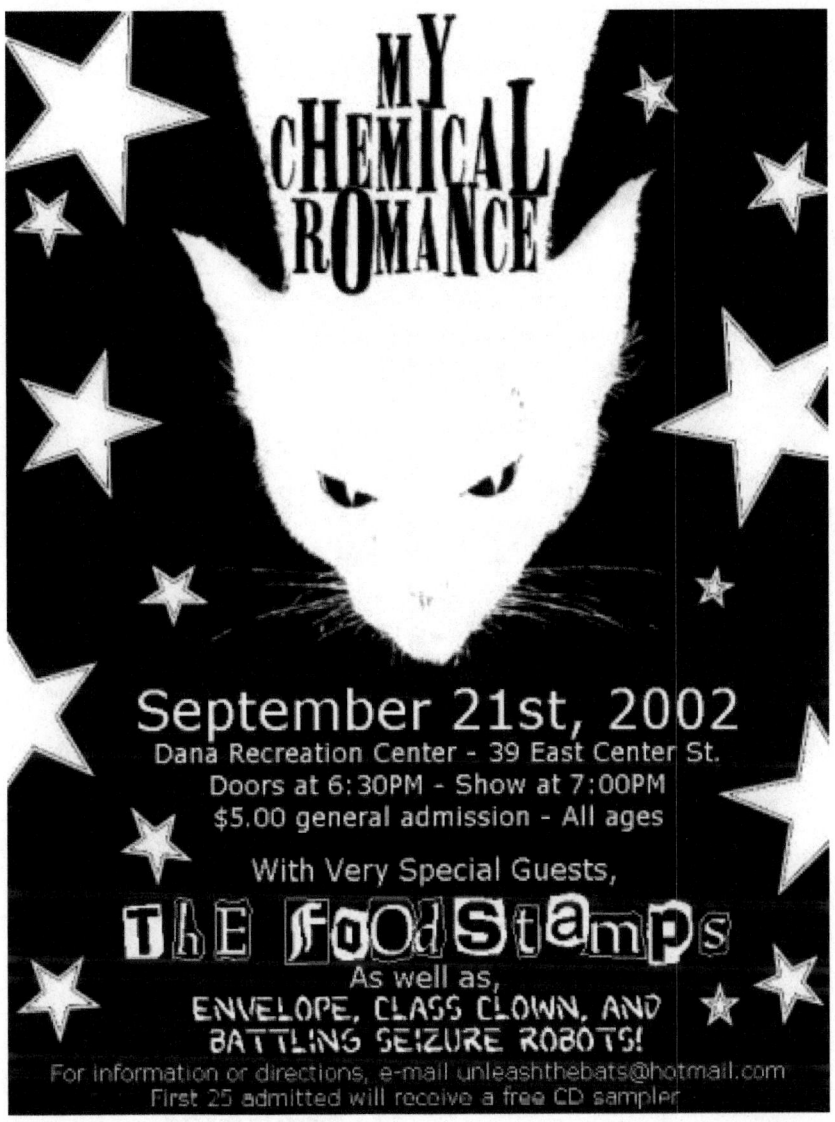

"Definitely '**Bullets...**'.
A lot of the album is sort of all over the place, talking about vampires, PTSD, and a girl that you had feelings for working in the cubicle near yours.
But the main reason why I love '**Bullets...**', is because the rawness of it. They said what they had to say, so straightforward. They didn't put out the album just to put out an album, they put it out because they felt like they needed to make a change by talking about real world problems in their music and yeah, it's their heaviest album. But I think that, and the

rawness was necessary to show the real sensitivity and emotion that was being talked about.
Another thing is that I love how it leads into their next album, **'Revenge...'**.
"The story of a man, a woman, and the corpses of a thousand evil men." The story of heartbreak, sorrow, and obviously, revenge (hence the album name).
I think that's why a lot of people love them.
MCR as a whole has gotten so many people through so much, because of things like being raw and straightforward.
But like I said, **'Bullets…'** is DEFINITELY my favorite!"
Julliana Jenkins (USA)

The Fans Have Their Say #15 My Chemical Romance

The Fans Have Their Say #15 My Chemical Romance

Three Cheers for Sweet Revenge

1) Helena……………………………………………………..……3:22
2) Give 'Em Hell, Kid…………………………………..……2:18
3) To the End……………………………………………….……3:01
4) You Know What They Do to Guys Like Us in Prison……...2:53
5) I'm Not Okay (I Promise)……………………………….……3:08
6) The Ghost of You……..……………………………….……3:22
7) The Jetset Life Is Gonna Kill You…………………….……3:37
8) Interlude…………………………………………………….0:57
9) Thank You for the Venom……..…………………….……..3:41
10) Hang 'Em High……………………………………….……2:47
11) It's Not a Fashion Statement, It's a Deathwish……..……3:30
12) Cemetary Drive……………………………………..……..3:08
13) I Never Told You What I Do For a Living………….…….3:51

Release Date: 8th June 2004
Producer: Howard Benson
Singles: 'I'm Not Okay (I Promise)',
'Thank You For the Venom', 'Helena'
'The Ghost of You'

The Fans Have Their Say #15 My Chemical Romance

"I still remember when I finally got my hands on this album...
My sister and I were on vacation visiting family in Guadalajara Jalisco, and we found a copy at the mall, and it was the last one! So, we begged our grandma to buy it for us and so the rest of our vacation was spent memorizing the lyrics and seeing who could have the entire album memorized first.
I'm sure my grandparents could sing along to some of the songs since we played it and sang along literally all the time.
I think the most significant gift that album gave me was a new thing of love with my sister; we're super close but that album brought us together during a dark time in our lives and we had been fighting so much (also we were 12 and 13 so we didn't need much to fight) and '**Three Cheers for Sweet Revenge**' gave us memories of dancing and singing together for an entire summer...and in October we're going to see them at The Forum in LA!"
Gina Jaqueline Brightside (Riverside, California, USA)

The Fans Have Their Say #15 My Chemical Romance

"I feel really happy and powerful when I listen to it. If it didn't exist, I don't think I would be happy with what I would listen to otherwise."
Lilly Youngs (In the World)

"The greatest concept album of all time."
Declan Edwards (Melbourne, Australia)

*"**Revenge…**' is my second favorite album for MCR (I fell in love with them through '**Danger Days**'.)*
*Growing up I was made fun of a lot for listening to the music my parents brought me up on (Metallica, Rush, Alice In Chains, Ozzy, etc.) and when I went home, the best way I found to fretted was blasting music on my computer. I would listen to '**Revenge…**' more than other albums when I had an especially bad day. It helped me a lot; it gave me an outlet for my anger at the time.*
Now, fun fact is I actually grew up and live IN the town Ray Toro is from, he went to prom with my high school photography teacher and went to the same high school I did. My dad knows his older brother!! So, I feel so connected to them, only being like 15 minutes away from where they formed in Newark.
My Chem, and this album helped me a lot.
It's the album I play in my car every morning before work; it's the album I resonate with the most. It's the album with mine and my best friend's favorite song.
I will forever love this album!"
Nicole McCarthy (Kearny, New Jersey, USA)

*"'**I'm Not Okay (I Promise)**' is forever going to be my anthem.*
It is soooo good, and I always listen to it whenever I'm feeling down, and it almost always cheers me up because of how rocky it is."
Jesse Slocum (USA)

"Absolutely amazing."
Archie Leach (Stockton-on-Tees, UK)

*"MCR's albums are amazing because they tell stories, I can't pick a favourite, but I love '**Revenge…**' so much. The music picks me up when I'm feeling down and is an outlet to express all the emotions."*
Jasmine Turner (Adelaide, Australia)

The Fans Have Their Say #15 My Chemical Romance

*"I love this album, not just the well-known songs like '**Helena**' or '**I'm Not Okay…**' or '**Ghost of You**' but the phrasing like Hotel Bella Murte or spun this chamber dry or talking about the changing color of the leaves or seasons change people don't.*
*I loved '**Bullets…**' as well but I feel like this album is where they found their sound."*
Elizabeth Jean (Paterson, New Jersey, USA)

"It's the best one. All are great, but that one is best."
Corey Oswald (Lansing, Michigan, USA)

The Fans Have Their Say #15 My Chemical Romance

"Good, not as great as 'The Black Parade' tho!"
Logan Langmead (Rhondda, Wales, UK)

"My brother and I first heard about My Chem when we would watch 'X-Play' and 'Attack of the Show' (nerdy video game review shows) on G4. Almost every commercial break, there would be the commercial for 'Three Cheers for Sweet Revenge'.
My brother and I got the album and immediately fell in love with it! 'Revenge...' later ended up getting me through junior high, as I was very ill most of the year and had about 15 brain surgeries in total. When I WAS in school, I was bullied for being in a wheelchair.
'Three Cheers for Sweet Revenge' taught me how to fight through one of the darkest times in my life and that it's okay to be different. To this day, it's still one of my favorite albums!
Jayne Mattingly (USA)

The Fans Have Their Say #15 My Chemical Romance

"I love all the songs and they all hit close to home. Especially 'Cemetery Drive', it reminds me of the people I've lost along the way."
Annabelle Cobb (UK)

The Fans Have Their Say #15 My Chemical Romance

"My first My Chemical Romance album.

I'll never forget avoiding watching the '**Helena**' video because I was a scared 13-year-old that just knew a dead girl came back to life and I could not deal so I changed the channel every time it came on.

Finally, one day I was lying in bed on a Sunday morning and the video came on and I didn't feel like getting up to get the remote, so I watched it and fell in love.

It was perfect.

The sound, the aesthetic, the perfectness went on to define my early teen years.

I remember being at Walmart and looking for the album (they don't sell parental advisory stuff I think) but while I was looking I all of a sudden heard '**Helena**' out of nowhere. It ended up being someone's ringtone, but I took it as a sign that I was destined to have this album and that it would be special.

The next day my brother's girlfriend surprised me with it before an 8hr road trip.

I listened to that album on repeat, on the road, on the hotel floor, during my brother's military graduation. I did not turn it off for weeks. It changed me in ways I can't even express.

Like I said it defined my early teenage years and continues to define me in different ways in my late 20's.

It will forever be my favorite album."

Gabriela Hawkins (Oklahoma City, Oklahoma, USA)

The Fans Have Their Say #15 My Chemical Romance

"Revenge…' when I feel alone, these songs that I always hear."
E'funniezt (Bandung, Indonesia)

"My favorite MCR album is *Three Cheers for Sweet Revenge* because the first song I listen to is *I'm Not Okay (I Promise)*."
Aaron Bazemore (Burlington, Vermont, USA)

The Fans Have Their Say #15 My Chemical Romance

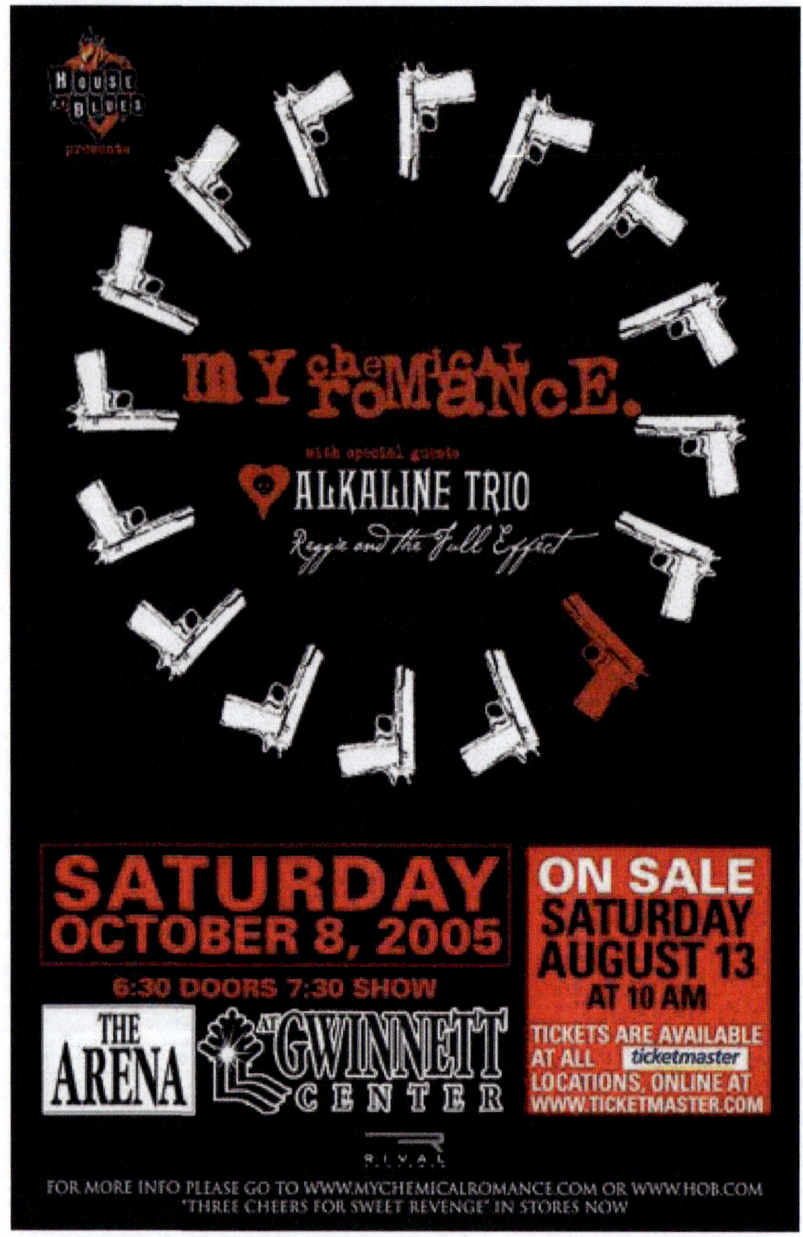

"*Three Cheers…*' came out when I was in high school. I didn't have the best upbringing and being an empath (and not knowing that at the time) I was very depressed. That album has got me through some of the tough times of my life. And has also somewhat predicted things to happen in my life. But I guess that's why I was drawn to them."
Nova Maples (Buffalo, Missouri, USA)

The Fans Have Their Say #15 My Chemical Romance

"Revenge...'."
Sonia Oliveira Libório (São Paulo, Brazil)

"Three Cheers...', it has more sad and heavy hitters but also bangers that you can jam to.
All around perfect album 10/10.
Favorite song is also *'Cemetery Drive'."*
Johnston Lastinger (USA)

"Three Cheers for Sweet Revenge'.
It's the album that my uncle constantly plays."
Sinang Del Pilar (In the World)

"Cause 'Ghost of You' and *'Cemetery Drive'* are my favourite songs of MCR.
With *'I'm Not Okay...'* I saw them the first on viva+ (German music television) and was totally in love."
Cindy Döll (Germany)

"Revenge...'."
Brandon Walls (Tipp City, Ohio, USA)

"Three Cheers...' I got the CD when I was 11 years old and I'm 27 now that album and band are still my all-time favorite *'Thank You for the Venom'* is my jam."
Paige Kelley (USA)

The Fans Have Their Say #15 My Chemical Romance

"*3 cheers...*' I loved their look and it got me thru the passings of people I love dearly."
Sylvie Gamboa (USA)

The Fans Have Their Say #15 My Chemical Romance

The Black Parade

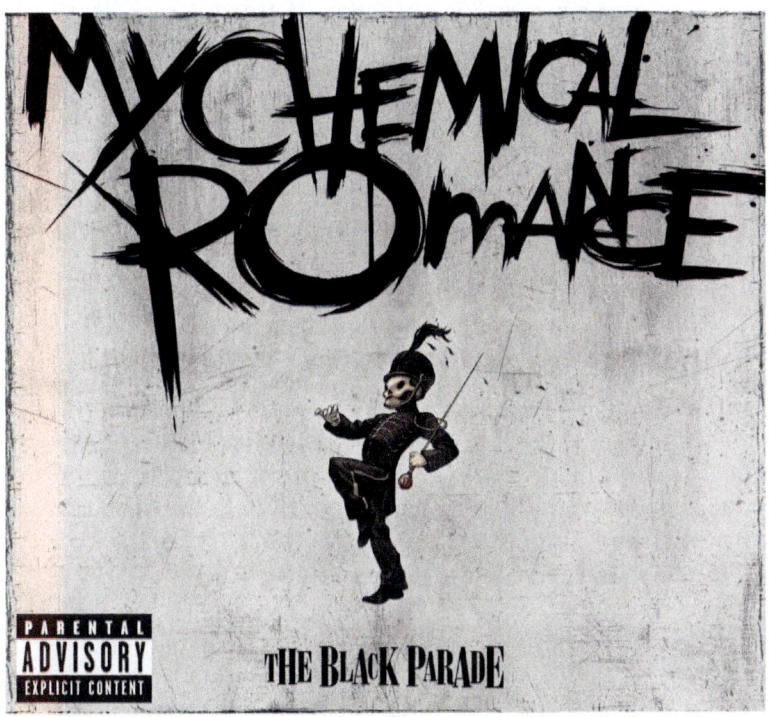

1) The End……………………………………………………1:02
2) Dead!………………………………………………………3:51
3) This Is How I Disappear…………………………………5:26
4) The Sharpest Lives………………………………………4:23
5) Welcome to the Black Parade…………………………2:05
6) I Don't Love You…………………………………………3:28
7) House of Wolves…………………………………………3:23
8) Cancer……………………………………………………5:04
9) Mama………………………………………………………2:12
10) Sleep………………………………………………………3:51
11) Teenagers…………………………………………………6:06
12) Disenchanted……………………………………………5:06
13) Famous Last Words……………………………………5:04
14) Blood………………………………………………………4:09

The Fans Have Their Say #15 My Chemical Romance

Release Date: 20th October 2006
Producer: Rob Cavallo, My Chemical Romance
Singles: 'Welcome to the Black Parade',
**   'Famous Last Words', 'I Don't Love You',**
**   'Teenagers'**

"**The Black Parade**', because of the 4, it is the only one that I consider totally relevant, the others have enough songs that go unnoticed by those who are fans of the band."
Rael Calunes (In the World)

"I'd have to go with '**the Black Parade**' although all of them are awesome.
The concept of the album is so good, and every song tells a different story of this man who is dying. Although my two favorite MCR songs are from '**Three Cheers for Sweet Revenge**', overall, I think '**the Black Parade**' is they're best album."
Isaiah McCain (In the World)

The Fans Have Their Say #15 My Chemical Romance

"*The Black Parade*' impacted me a lot and helped me through a few bad times."
Zach O'Brien (In the World)

The Fans Have Their Say #15 My Chemical Romance

*"**The Black Parade**' cuz of the g note, lol."*
George Sussex (Bideford, Devon, UK)

The Fans Have Their Say #15 My Chemical Romance

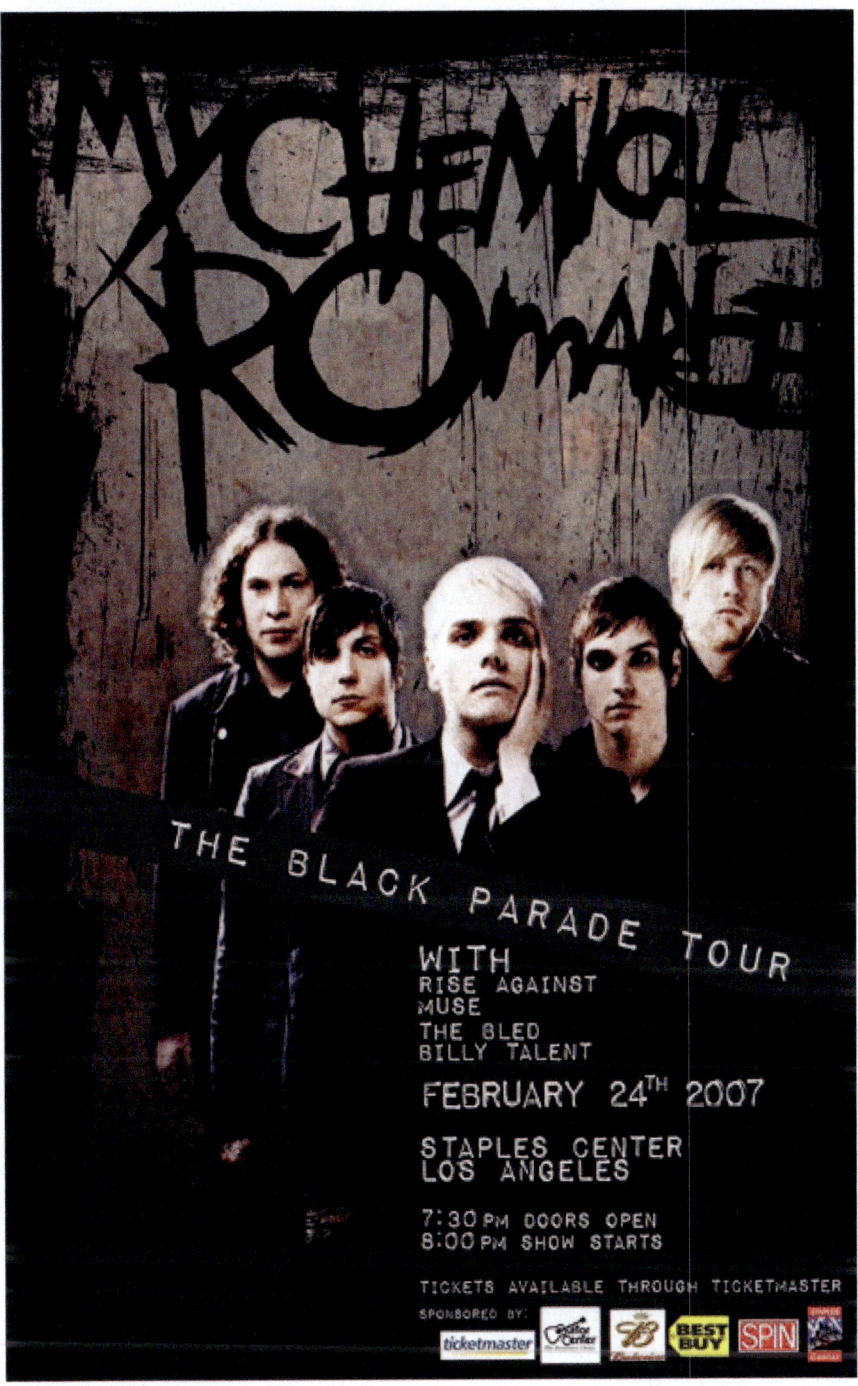

"Black Parade'!"
Rebekah Ami Briggs (UK)

The Fans Have Their Say #15 My Chemical Romance

*"I would have to go with '**The Black Parade**' because the album is really good, and every song is telling a story about the man who is dying and over all the album is just really good but don't get me wrong all the other albums are really good too."*
Adrynna Powell (In the World)

*"I used to have long car commutes with a music savvy friend who introduced me to the '**Three Cheers…**' album; absolutely nothing passed the time better than shouting your brains out to each one of those songs. A few months later, '**Welcome to the Black Parade**' came out on the radio and hearing it for the first time I wondered,*
"What the hell did I just listen to!???"
*Naturally, I bought '**The Black Parade**' CD and being a huge sucker for sing-along ballads, that album was just beyond 'it' for me.*
Strangely though, I felt uncomfortable being so drawn to MCR; it was a brand-new type of music for me that just was so different and I didn't know what to make of it.
Another oddity is that for 2-3 years, I never bothered to look up anything about MCR. Then one day, I was in a record store, and I grabbed an MCR poster.
When I finally hung it up, I couldn't help but notice the dude in front was fairly attractive.
I busted out my laptop and this was the first time I had ever checked the internet for MCR content, including videos. Definitely, I was disappointed to learn this 'Gerard guy' was married.
At any rate, whatever my fascination was with them I do know that it had nothing to do with the EMO scene or hot Jersey boys, it was just their captivating music that bewitched me.
With a new generation of fans from all around the world, it is apparent their artistry has withstood the test of time. Everything they touch to this day is still in demand and I wonder at what point did MCR realize they had created monster."
Hayley Mann (USA)

The Fans Have Their Say #15 My Chemical Romance

*"I love '**The Black Parade**' because first of all it's the first one I ever heard, but second of all because it has all this emotion in the songs and tells a story.*
It's so powerful and amazing!"
Kaitlyn Marini (Abington, Massachusetts, USA)

The Fans Have Their Say #15 My Chemical Romance

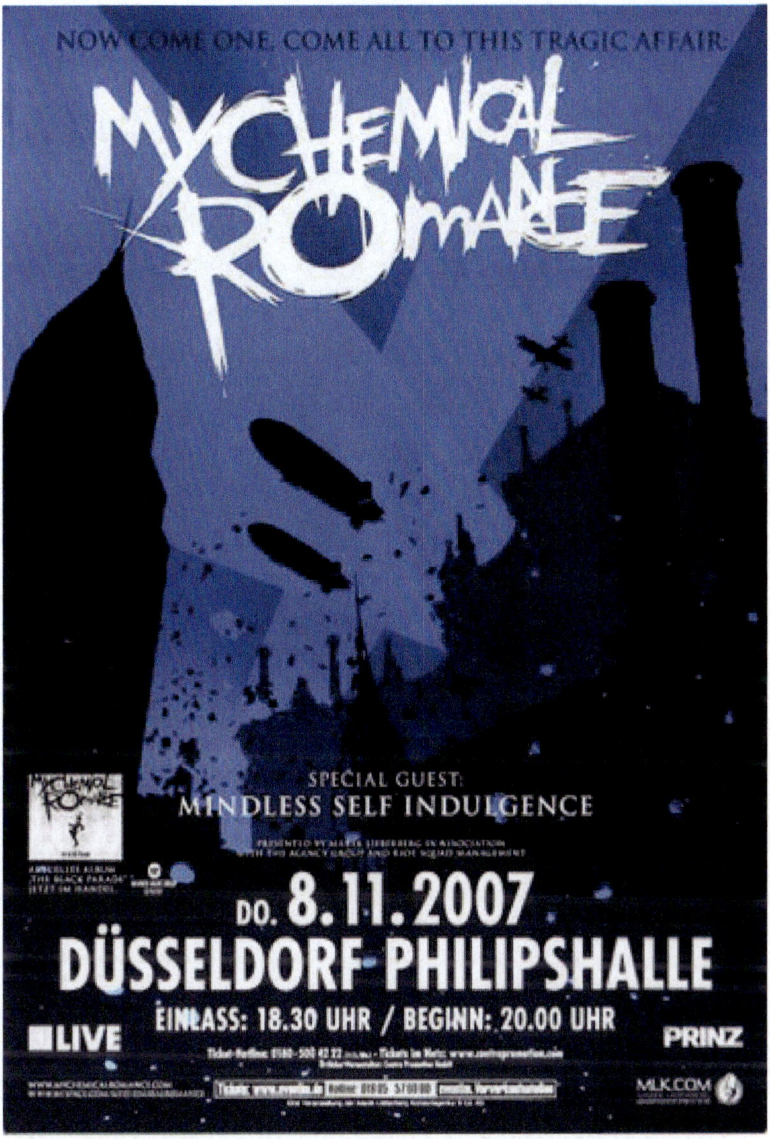

The Fans Have Their Say #15 My Chemical Romance

The Fans Have Their Say #15 My Chemical Romance

Danger Days:
The True Lives of the Fabulous Killjoys

1) Look Alive, Sunshine………………………………………0:29
2) Na Na Na (Na Na Na Na Na Na Na Na Na)………………..3:25
3) Bulletproof Heart…………………………………………..4:55
4) Sing…………………………………………………………4:29
5) Planetary (Go!)……………………………………………..4:06
6) The Only Hope for Me Is You……………………………...4:32
7) Jet-Star and the Kobra Kid/Traffic Report……………….. 0:26
8) Part Poison………………………………………………….3:35
9) Save Yourself, I'll Hold Them Back……………………….3:49
10) S/C/A/R/E/C/R/O/W……………………………………...4:27
11) Summertime……………………………………………….4:06
12) Destroya…………………………………………………...4:32
13) The Kids from Yesterday………………………………….5:24
14) Goodnite, Dr. Death……………………………………….1:58
15) Vampire Money……………………………………………3:37

The Fans Have Their Say #15 My Chemical Romance

Release Date: 22nd November 2010
Producer: Rob Cavallo, My Chemical Romance
Singles: 'Na Na Na (Na Na Na Na Na Na Na Na)', 'The Only Hope for Me Is You', 'Sing', 'Planetary (Go!)', 'Bulletproof Heart', 'The Kids from Yesterday'

*"I like **Danger Days** a lot, but it really depends."*
Zack O'Brien (In the World)

The Fans Have Their Say #15 My Chemical Romance

 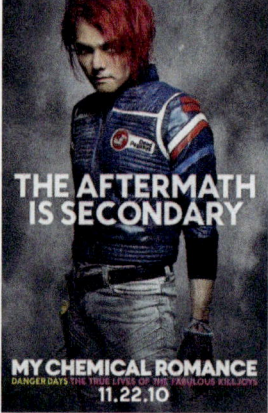 

The Fans Have Their Say #15 My Chemical Romance

"I lost touch with MCR during the time between '**The Black Parade**' and '**Danger Days**'.
The next thing you know, MCR broke up and somehow this affected me on a deep level; it was really depressing listening to '**3 Cheers…**' and '**TBP**' music. But just as Ray, Frank, Mikey, and Gerard 'carried on' in their lives, I had to as well.
However, when MCR started hinting at a reunion tour, my inner-MCR child rapidly emerged; but this time, it was with a vengeance. I found myself listening, watching and reading everything I could MCR-related. Being a grown ass adult with a career job, I also dropped some serious bank on reunion concert tickets.
I even decided I wanted to start playing guitar. I didn't know what guitar to buy, so I turned to Frank for inspiration; amazingly, I managed to buy Frank's signature 2011 Epiphone guitar (to this day, it is waiting for me in Canada thanks to the pandemic-related border closure and me being stubborn about shipping).

The Fans Have Their Say #15 My Chemical Romance

But allow me to backtrack a bit; I had never listened to the entire '**Danger Days**' album before and truthfully, I found it difficult (I'm also not such a fan of comics).

However, this was reminiscent of my usual reaction to new MCR music, so I wasn't deterred.

I began to realize that '**Danger Days**' was actually a fairly respectable Rock n' Roll-type album.

I found myself listening to it daily.

On a larger note, I strongly believe that MCR has never received the praise they deserve from 'official industry entities' (e.g., Grammy's). Why is that? Could it be that there wasn't a mainstream genre that defined them? Or maybe they scared all the grown-ups with their horror makeup and 'devil worshipping'? Seriously though, I think that alternative music is just highly under-appreciated in general.

However, with MCR's music hitting charts again and the reunion tour selling out worldwide within minutes, it will be extremely hard to not acknowledge that MCR is a real music industry force. Rolling Stone did recently place '**The Black Parade**' within the top 500 best albums of all time, but that's still nowhere near the recognition they deserve.

Finally, to conclude, if anyone ever says, '**Danger Days**' is not good, then they're simply just the wrong kind of Killjoy."

Hayley Mann (USA)

The Fans Have Their Say #15 My Chemical Romance

"***Danger Days*** *coz it kinda helped me come out and be more expressive towards the world in a way.*"
Aush Bomjan (Siliguri, India)

The Fans Have Their Say #15 My Chemical Romance

The Fans Have Their Say #15 My Chemical Romance

Iceland

"My Chemical Romance has helped me through a lot and will probably continue to do so for the rest of my life.
Their music showcases and at the same time cures the emotions and problems I have had to face. Along with those emotions there are interesting stories woven into the songs.
The members of the band are truly amazing people and inspire us all to take no shit, be creative and most importantly be ourselves."
Hervör F. Hjörvarsdóttir (Skagafjörður, Iceland)

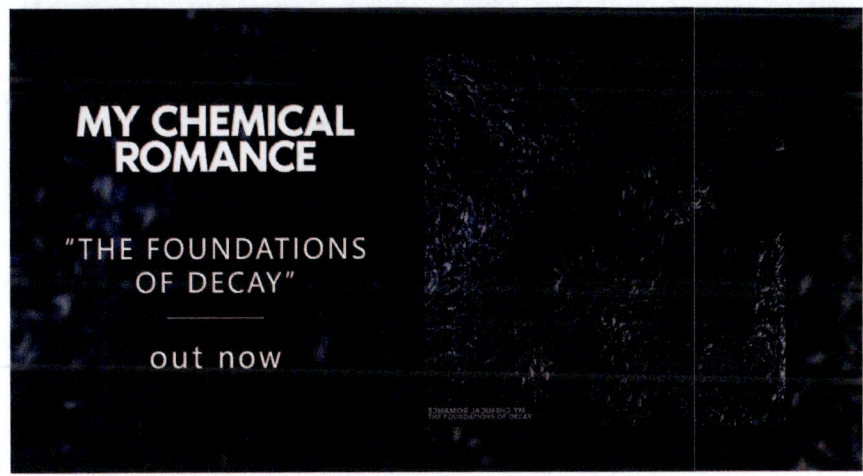

The Fans Have Their Say #15 My Chemical Romance

In the World

"I haven't been to a show YET, but if I did, I could die happily."
Lilly Youngs (In the World)

*"**The Black Parade is Dead**' live in Mexico City. Crazy awesome concert only wish I could have been there."*
Isaiah McCain (In the World)

The Fans Have Their Say #15 My Chemical Romance

Mexico

"Difícil decisión entre, *'Three Cheers For Sweet Revenge'* y *'I Brought You My Bullets You Brought Me Your Love'*."
Jaazz Mndz (Mexico)

The Fans Have Their Say #15 My Chemical Romance

New Zealand

"Easy it will be 25/03/20 here in New Zealand at Western Springs Stadium, my first time seeing them after 14 years of obsession and love for them.
I still remember the night of their concert here in 2007 and I spent the whole night listening to '**TBP**' on repeat crying in my room at my grandma's. This concert is going to make my whole life."
Magenta Roimata Mudgway (Wellington)

The Fans Have Their Say #15 My Chemical Romance

United Kingdom

"Liverpool University before they became massive in Britain. Small venue and it was f*cking madness. Best gig I've ever been to."
Alexandra Westwell (Merseyside)

*"21/02/2011- Cardiff International Arena. '****World Contamination Tour****'. I was lucky enough to see My Chemical Romance two days before my 14th birthday, along with my sister and mum who are also massive fans too.*
We travelled by train from Torquay to Cardiff.
The whole day felt so surreal and weird, like none of it was really happening. I just couldn't believe I was only a few hours away from seeing My Chemical Romance!
As we started walking towards the venue my sister took us straight to the box office, bypassing the already giant queue, I had no idea what she was doing. Then she told me she had a birthday surprise for me, she had upgraded all our tickets to get early entry into the venue and a meal inside before the show.
As I was standing waiting in line for our early entry, it all suddenly became so real.
I could feel myself getting emotional but didn't want to cry in front of everyone, so I turned away and tried my hardest to hold back my tears. My sister asked me if I was okay, and all the tears just burst out and I sobbed –
"I'm just so happy!"
*The show was so brightly coloured and amazing, it really embodied what the '****Danger Days****' album was all about. I especially loved the montage of*

'Danger Days' photos and quotes that flashed up on the screen before the band started playing.

After the show I waited around to see if the band would come out. After a long wait a security member came out and asked everybody to get into a queue as Gerard, Frank and Ray were about to come out to sign our stuff. The rules were no photos, no screaming and only one item to sign. As we got closer to the band I was shaking and could feel my heart beating so fast, one of the security members even asked if I was going to be okay!

Months before the show I had hand stitched a little black pillow with the My Chemical Romance logo sewn on, when I got up to Gerard, I handed it to him and told him I had made it for the band. He said it was awesome and then signed my ticket. I remember Frank having a massive smile the whole time and Ray thanked us for coming to see them play.

It really was an amazing experience seeing the band I've loved so much for so long. I even got the numbers 005796 tattooed on my wrist as that was the number printed on my wristband.

Brianna Bam Killjoy (Torquay)

Cardiff International Arena, Cardiff, 'World Contamination' Tour, 21st February 2011

Na Na Na (Na Na Na Na Na Na Na Na Na)
Give 'Em Hell Kid
Planetary (GO!)
You Know What They Do to Guys Like Us in Prison
SING
Vampire Money
Mama
The Only Hope for Me is You
Summertime
I'm Not Okay (I Promise)
Famous Last Words
DESTROYA
Welcome to the Black Parade
Teenagers
Helena
Cancer
Bulletproof Heart

The Fans Have Their Say #15 My Chemical Romance

"The first boy I was in love with, we went to an MCR gig when we were underage and smuggled in vodka. We slow danced to *'Ghost of You'*. I've been proposed to multiple times and that was still the most romantic moment of my life."
Natalie Hance (London)

The Fans Have Their Say #15 My Chemical Romance

*"The tour where they played '**The Black Parade**' from start to finish then got changed and banged out hits from their first two, is one of the best gigs I have ever witnessed."*
Craig Asson (Great Barr, Walsall)

(More Cancelled Shows Due to COVID-19)

The Fans Have Their Say #15 My Chemical Romance

"I first saw MCR at the Download Festival in 2005, they were 3rd from top in the tent playing after Inme and just before the Used, on a night that was headlined by Billy Idol.
Gerard played the set – to a tightly packed crowd – in a full-on body vest adding to the standout performance of the night.

Download Festival, Donington Park, UK 10th June 2005

Helena
Cemetery Drive
Thank You for the Venom
Honey, This Mirror Ain't Big Enough for the Two of Us
To the End
Give 'Em Hell Kid
Our Lady of Sorrows
You Know What They Do to Guys Like Us in Prison
I'm Not Okay (I Promise)

The Fans Have Their Say #15 My Chemical Romance

The Fans Have Their Say #15 My Chemical Romance

This set was an amazing introduction to all things MCR and the next time at Download Festival (2007) was to be even more special.

My wife was very ill at the time, going in and out of hospital with cancer. Our son at the time was only 9 (he's 24 now) and as he couldn't stay in Plymouth whilst his mum was poorly, he came away with us to his first Download Festival.

He was interviewed as well by Scuzz TV and that truly made his day and made me extremely proud of him – the following year at Download, someone came up to and asked him if he was the young boy off the TV!"

Ian Carroll (Plymouth, Devon)

The Fans Have Their Say #15 My Chemical Romance

Download Festival, Donington Park, UK 8th June 2005

Dead!
This Is How I Disappear
I'm Not Okay (I Promise)
Cemetery Drive
The Sharpest Lives
Welcome to the Black Parade
I Don't Love You
Give 'Em Hell Kid
House of Wolves
Teenagers
Cancer
You Know What They Do to Guys Like Us in Prison
Sleep
Mama
Famous Last Words
Helena

The Fans Have Their Say #15 My Chemical Romance

United States of America

"Been wanting to since 2003. Still haven't seen them."
Julia Jaén (Florida, USA)

"When I was in eighth grade in San Antonio, Texas - my parents bought myself and them tickets to see **'the Black Parade'** *tour.*
Now this was the night before a really big test that we had to take in middle school in Texas and it was the math one, so I was extremely nervous. Now my parents haven't always been super supportive, but they knew how badly I wanted to see them, and I was able to convince them to take me, but they were gonna be my chaperones.
Now the day of the concert, my parents bought themselves My Chemical Romance shirts and they bought me a brand new one as well as brand new shoes.
Now, we get to the concert venue and as were standing outside my mom and my dad are talking about a shooting that had taken place in Virginia at the University earlier that day.
The concert was amazing, and I cried 1001 times and it was everything to my heart's content and I remember the band taking a moment of silence to honor the victims of the shooting.
When we left the venue, my dad put his arm around me and he said,
"You know I never really understood why you liked those boys that much but that was very respectful of them, and I'm surprised at how much they sound exactly like the album."
Best memory ever."
Krystal Estrada (Universal City, Texas)

The Fans Have Their Say #15 My Chemical Romance

"I've seen My Chemical Romance live six times, and each was its own amazing experience. But the most memorable was last year (2019), the reunion show.

Hearing the news of the return and managing to get a ticket happened so fast that it didn't feel like it was real. I found myself in Los Angeles the day before the show, and '**Helena**' started playing. That's when it set in, and I couldn't help but cry.

The next day I got to the Shrine early and stood alone in line for hours. Friends of mine knew how important this was to me, and I got texts throughout the day hoping I was having a good time, and even in that line I truly was.

The first wave of endorphins came when they started letting people in. I got myself to the middle of the floor, as close to the front as possible.

The second wave came after Thursday (the band) finished.

The room was buzzing as the curtain hung in front of the stage, but once the music cut off there was a collective gasp. The energy built and everyone's eyes were staring forward in extreme anticipation.

The first notes of '**I'm Not Okay (I Promise)**' began and the most beautiful moment of my life happened. A moment I never was sure would happen again.

A complete and amazing set by my favorite band.

Every song bellowing from the mouths of hundreds of people in various states of emotion.

The gratitude flowed both ways that night and by the end of it all there was a heavy happiness enveloping us all.

I will never forget that night and I'm forever grateful I got to be there for that."

Sarah Dineen (Las Vegas, Nevada)

The Fans Have Their Say #15 My Chemical Romance

Shrine Expo Hall, Los Angeles, California 'Return' show, 20th December 2019

I'm Not Okay (I Promise)
Thank You for the Venom
Give 'Em Hell Kid
House of Wolves
Summertime
You Know What They Do to Guys Like Us in Prison
Make Room!!!!
Our Lady of Sorrows
Na Na Na (Na Na Na Na Na Na Na Na Na)
Sleep
Mama
I Don't Love You
DESTROYA
Teenagers
S/C/A/R/E/C/R/O/W
Famous Last Words
The Kids from Yesterday
Vampire Money
Helena
Welcome to the Black Parade

The Fans Have Their Say #15 My Chemical Romance

*"My very first concert ever in 2005 in Ypsilanti, Michigan.
I was in 8th grade and waited outside forever with a friend and my mom.
I got to the bar just in front of Frank.
Aiden opened for them.
I was so young I can't remember much but I do remember it changed my life to see my heroes."*
Ashley Osborn (Flint, Michigan, USA)

*"2007 Edgefest in Dallas was my first show.
My older brother took me and bravely followed me into the pit to get as close as possible. I think I came close to passing out a couple times because it was so intense, but it was so perfect.
Second, was HOB Dallas, 2011.
I went with my two best friends. Unfortunately, they weren't as hardcore fans as me and wanted to stay in the back. That's when I ventured alone to the very front and center.
It was a magical experience. And I got a pick from Mikey!!!"*
Gabriela Hawkins (Oklahoma City, Oklahoma, USA)

*"**Danger Days**' album premier."*
Jackson Phillips (East Rockingham, North Carolina)

*"05/10/2011 9:30 Club Washington D.C.
This club only holds 1,200 people and sold out in SECONDS. I was only able to get tickets by refreshing and I got extremely lucky.
Keep in mind even on this tour they were playing at 5,000 people + venues so the fact that we got a somewhat intimate club show was pure magic.
There was not one person there that was apathetic or just tagging along with a friend, this was one of the only shows I've been to where the crowd was 100% invested.
It felt like there was electricity in the air and when '**Look Alive Sunshine**' came on before the curtain dropped chaos ensued.
The whole show just felt electric and after going to over 100 shows I haven't experienced something like it since.
This band means a lot to its fans; the MCRmy is a beast on its own, that's fiercely loyal to the band and other fans. It's something I was proud to be a part of 10 years ago, and I'm proud to be a part of it now. Having seen them in a 1000-person venue to now counting down the days to Sept 22nd at 19,000 and having them both sell out just as quickly, 10 years apart says something about MCR and about the fans."*
Kayleigh Skellington (Chambersburg, Pennsylvania, USA)

The Fans Have Their Say #15 My Chemical Romance

9:30 Club, Washington
'World Contamination' Tour, 10th May 2011

Na Na Na (Na Na Na Na Na Na Na Na Na)
Thank You for the Venom
Planetary (GO!)
Hang 'Em High
Mama
The Only Hope for Me is You
House of Wolves
Summertime
I'm Not Okay (I Promise)
Vampire Money
DESTROYA
Welcome to the Black Parade
Teenagers
SING
Vampires Will Never Hurt You
Helena
Cancer
Our Lady of Sorrows
Bulletproof Heart

"Saw them for the first time for my birthday. They were absolutely incredible. It was my first concert and I'm so excited that I get to experience that all over again this year!"
Bri Patton (Denver, Colorado, USA)

"I've only been to one show so far. It was in 2010, but it was amazing. The atmosphere was magical. There was a palpable feeling of unity.
We were all there for the same reason. We had a band we adore, and we wouldn't want to be anywhere else that night.
It was at the Fillmore in Detroit. The balcony I was watching from was literally SWAYING with the people on it. It felt like the thing could collapse at any moment, but honestly, we would die happy lol."
Luke Bossio (USA)

The Fans Have Their Say #15 My Chemical Romance

"Top 2:
1) MSG concert. Just an overall beautiful experience. They kept talking about how surreal it was to play at the venue Gerard and Mikey saw The Smashing Pumpkins play years ago. It was just an incredible night. And my dad paid a security guard to move us from way back to the section right next to the stage - it was dope
2) Starland Ballroom in NJ. '*Danger Days*' tour - awesome to see them in an intimate venue. They played '*Vampires...*' and it fucking SLAPPED. That was an awesome show, loud, sweaty, and beautiful." **Eric Glauber (New Paltz, New York)**

"I was lucky enough to see MCR perform three times from 2006-2010, this picture was taken in 2008.
They changed my life, made me fearless to be myself.
Inspired me to be an artist and literally gave me the will to keep on living. I could not be more thankful for the venom and so happy to see their continued success."
Estefania Vanyi (Beaverton, Oregon)

The Fans Have Their Say #15 My Chemical Romance

*"I first heard My Chemical Romance back in 2006, I believe. I was about ten years old. I was on my way to school, and '**Teenagers**' came on the radio. I thought it was catchy, but that was really about it.*

Then, in 2007, I lost my uncle who was my best friend. I quickly spiralled downward into depression and anxiety.

*The day of his funeral, I heard '**Welcome to the Black Parade**'; the song just seemed so fitting.*

Once I had gone home, I began looking up some of their other music, and before I knew it, I was in love. Even at only eleven years old, these guys managed to connect with me on an emotional level.

Their music and their interviews and their behind-the-scenes videos got me through one of the hardest parts of my life.

That was the first time they saved my life.

Then, in high school, I got into a pretty messy situation. I got on drugs, started drinking excessively, and just generally not taking care of myself. By the time I was in tenth grade, I had hit my bottom. I attempted suicide. Thankfully, it didn't go the way that I had planned.

*While I was in the hospital, I was listening to my music, and '**Famous Last Words**' came on.*

That song hit me a lot differently than it had in the previous years. So, that day, I decided I was going to get my life together. I quit drinking, quit doing drugs. I was better.

That was the second time they saved my life.

Then, in 2018, my worst nightmare come true. I lost my best friend.

She was the only one who had stayed with me through all of my shit. That broke me. I got really depressed again, and I started drinking.

*I was on my way to meet someone for some drugs, and the craziest thing happened. My phone decided to glitch, played music from an old playlist, and it just so happened that the song that came on was '**Famous Last Words**.' That was the third time they saved my life.*

A lot of people don't understand why I'm 'obsessed' with those guys.

I'm constantly told that it's just a band, or that I am over exaggerating when I say that they saved my life. In all reality, I wouldn't have been able to make it through those parts of my life without them.

I guess I really just want them to know that they accomplished what they set out to do. They have saved my life, and I know that there are thousands of others who will say the same. If they can have that kind of impact on people of all ages, there isn't a thing in this world that they can't do.

Jasmine Jacobs (USA)

The Fans Have Their Say #15 My Chemical Romance

*"I've only seen them once, on 5/4/08, but I'll never forget the show starting with the opening riff of '**Give 'Em Hell, Kid**' or Gerard screaming, "Columbus, Ohio!" to a cheering audience.*
I jumped and yelled so hard that I had to sit down because I almost passed out, but it was a magical night. And because I'm such a smart person, I went deep and dumb when I met Frank that night, and I asked him to sign my cell phone instead of the ticket in my back pocket. Absolutely unforgettable."
Ashley Nicole Labaki (USA)

(Another cancelled appearance due to the COVID-19 Pandemic)

The Fans Have Their Say #15 My Chemical Romance

"I became a fan in 2005, one morning I was getting ready for school and *Helena* came up in the TV, I fell in love.
Then a few months after, I was trying to disappear, when I was self-harming myself the video for *'I'm Not Okay…'* appeared on MTV, I felt like someone was telling me that they knew how it felt - what I was feeling - that moment they saved my life.

The Fans Have Their Say #15 My Chemical Romance

Everytime that something has happened, and I try to disappear they are there.
Next year (hopefully) if it doesn't get postponed, I will be seeing them for the very first time live here in Las Vegas, that's my #1 band in my list that I never thought I would get to see.
I finally got my most desired concert ticket.
And to be honest, everyone who knows me knows that when I see them that will change my life forever because they saved my life, without them I wouldn't be here with my full-time job, newlywed to a MCR fan haha and in my last year in college. All thanks to the guys. MCR fan forever and ever."

Maria Chiang Lopez (Las Vegas, Nevada)

The Fans Have Their Say #15 My Chemical Romance

UK & European Tour 2022 Memories

The Fans Have Their Say #15 My Chemical Romance

Gerard Way at the Eden Project 17th May 2022

The Fans Have Their Say #15 My Chemical Romance

"Unfortunately, when I was into MCR originally, I was too young to go to one of their concerts and following the news of their break I thought I'd never be able to have the experience. When I heard, they were coming to the UK for the first time in 10 years I cried of happiness.
During my teenage years, I went through a lot, and considered taking my life almost every day. My Chemical Romance along with a couple other bands really helped me through this and are truly the reason why I'm still alive today.
Before MCR came on stage it didn't feel real but the second they walked out my heart sank as I was finally seeing the people who saved my life. I got very emotional but held back tears.
As soon as the Chorus of '**Famous Last Words**' started, I started bawling my eyes out, I'm not afraid to keep on living BECAUSE of this band. They've helped me in so many ways and they don't even know me.
For future tours I would love for them to do meet and greets, I would love to get an autograph so I can get it tattooed one day to remind me that I am strong enough and to remind me how much I've overcome. Words simply cannot describe how much these guys helped me without knowing it and I know I'm not the only one. For this I'd like to say thank you, although I'll probably never get the chance to tell them this.
I really do hope they know how much they've helped us all."
Eboni Primett (Sittingbourne, UK)

"I've been a fan since 2004 when I was 14 years old. There has always been a reason to why I haven't been able to see My Chemical Romance live. But this year at the age of 32, I finally managed to see them.
It was such an emotional experience. From the moment they came on stage. The sound of the crowd just added to the experience. Just amazing.
I hope I can take my daughter to the next tour as unfortunately I couldn't afford it this time round. She's a big fan too."
Julia Elizabeth Chiarello (Coventry, UK)

The Fans Have Their Say #15 My Chemical Romance

Eden Sessions, St. Austell, Cornwall 16th May 2022

The Foundations of Decay
Helena
Give 'Em Hell Kid
Make Room!!!!
Summertime
This Is How I Disappear
You Know What They Do to Guys Like Us in Prison
Na Na Na (Na Na Na Na Na Na Na Na Na)
Famous Last Words
Surrender the Night
Teenagers
DESTROYA
Our Lady of Sorrows
Vampire Money
Thank You for the Venom
Mama
Welcome to the Black Parade
Sleep
Boy Division
I'm Not Okay (I Promise)
The Kids from Yesterday

"When they played '**Famous Last Words**' the tears streamed... at 34 years old I wish I could've told my 18-year-old self that I would be alright and that that song would get me through. I cannot put into words what it meant to me and what it meant to experience it live.
Now I have my children and my beautiful 6-year-old daughter is in Love with MCR. After I came back from MK and for my birthday (which is today) she sang '*Helena*' for me.
My heart is so happy to share that with her."
Emma Louise (UK)

The Fans Have Their Say #15 My Chemical Romance

"Me and my friend Marie arrived at the venue at MK on the 19th May at Gate 5 at about 2pm.
We were greeted by some fans who welcomed us to the 'Emo Line' - we sat for an hour just getting more and more excited for the gig. Then I decided to go get food from the nearby Asda and meet up with my long-time friend Brodie from Yorkshire for a brief preshow catch up.
I brought my tour t-shirt and returned to the line now with added noodles and sushi!
On arrival I say how much I'm loving my food, which a person with green hair who I would later learn was called Kayleigh shouted "I love your energy"- anyway it was from that moment we ended up chatting and bonding with her, David, Fern and Amber and 5 mins later Fern was adding a temporary tattoo of a dragon to my face. We all looked around all face tattooed and smiled.

The Fans Have Their Say #15 My Chemical Romance

We were now an MCR crew, even having just met.

Shortly after Security came over to us saying that we had to move from this gate after we are let in. But as an apology they would give us and the next 1000 people a free upgrade to 'golden circle' aka FRONT PIT! We all couldn't believe our luck at our dream gig we were gonna be at the front to see My Chemical Romance. We all got through the gates. Took each other's Instagram and arranged to all stand together in the 'golden circle'.

The doors opened at Gate 3, and we rushed into the Venue. Everyone in my newly established crew clinging onto me - as I'm 6ft 5" - so we didn't get separated in the rush. I felt like Eren from 'Attack on Titan' or Gandalf from 'Lord of The Rings' leading his fellowship.

Anyway, we made it to the 'golden circle' (front pit) we all positioned ourselves to the right of the stage and began to wait for the first support at

Witch Fever' when they arrived on stage, we became instant fans. They were freaking awesome and a lot of fun to watch.

The other support act LostAlone we all found a bit annoying with the amount of audience interaction they wanted. Dude we are waiting to use our energy on MCR! It was just before Placebo my friend Sophulla rang me telling me she had arrived. "Oh, crap I thought... She doesn't have golden circle' anyway long story short and I'm sorry MK, but I managed to peel off my MCR gold circle wrist band carefully covering up I didn't have it on with my hoodie. Gave it to Kayleigh who had never met Sophulla before. To deliver it to Sophulla in the ladies' toilets. It was like something out of 'Mission Impossible'. Lucky Sophulla happened to have blister plasters to stick it together with. As we all waited for bated breath to see if it would work or would security notice the band had been ripped and fixed...

 Minutes past when eventually Sophulla arrived with Kayleigh. We all cheered as I threw my arms round Sophulla. The squad was completed we were all ready for MCR.

We had all expected to see Gerard appear in his standard 'Oasis' inspired look. When suddenly to our surprise he comes out in a MASKED BLOODY SUIT! we were all stunned and honestly excited at this almost Three Cheers call-back. He roared into '**The Foundations of Decay**' and from that moment we all knew we were in for something extremely special!

Throughout the night we would all sing our hearts out. We would laugh, cry, and smile. Not only was it an incredible gig I'll never forget I gained friends for life attending it!

THANK YOU MCR FOR THIS SPECIAL NIGHT!"

Chris Josty (Newport, Wales, UK)

The Fans Have Their Say #15 My Chemical Romance

Eden Sessions, St. Austell, Cornwall 17th May 2022

The Foundations of Decay
Helena
Give 'Em Hell Kid
Cemetery Drive
The Only Hope for Me is You
Boy Division
House of Wolves
Na Na Na (Na Na Na Na Na Na Na Na Na)
Welcome to the Black Parade
Teenagers
The Ghost of You
DESTROYA
Surrender the Night
Vampire Money
Thank You for the Venom
Mama
S/C/A/R/E/C/R/O/W
Famous Last Words
Headfirst for Halos
Mastas of Ravencroft
I'm Not Okay (I Promise)
The Kids From Yesterday

"I was there on the 22nd in Milton Keynes.
When Gerard played '**Cancer**' I cried, I had to turn into my boyfriend for a hug. This band had saved my life a few years prior - it was something I needed.
I feel alive."
Sophie Devlin (Birmingham, UK)

The Fans Have Their Say #15 My Chemical Romance

Stadium MK, Milton Keynes, UK 19th May 2022

The Foundations of Decay
Helena
Give 'Em Hell Kid
Make Room!!!!
Teenagers
Summertime
The Only Hope for Me is You
Boy Division
DESTROYA
Na Na Na (Na Na Na Na Na Na Na Na Na)
Welcome to the Black Parade
The Ghost of You
It's Not a Fashion Statement, It's a Fucking Deathwish
Thank You for the Venom
Mama
Famous Last Words
The Kids From Yesterday
Skylines and Turnstiles
Mastas of Ravencroft
I'm Not Okay (I Promise)
Goodnite Dr. Death
Vampire Money

The Fans Have Their Say #15 My Chemical Romance

*"My Chemical Romance has got me through the darkest times of my life, I first heard '**I'm Not Okay**' back when I was in year 4 but didn't become fully obsessed until I was about 11.*
Their music will always sound so comforting to me, they feel like home. Each and every one of their songs has a special place in my heart. I could never have imagined just how incredible it would be to see them live. I can't remember a lot from when I was younger but going to see them has been a dream of mine since I first heard them, it just never felt possible. I want to say I was living my younger self's dream but really that still was my dream. I have never grown out of my love for this band, and I never will.
Being so close to them last night, seeing them as real people and just getting to experience it all was the most therapeutic thing. My Chemical Romance saved my life, they got me through everything life has thrown at me, when it's been bad, I listened to them and kept going, when it was good, I listened to them and celebrated. Last night was healing. That really unlocked some deep buried trauma and emotions for me to just let go off.
I would never have made it to today if it wasn't for them, their music and who they are as people. I just really don't have the words to describe what that gig was and how much it meant to me, I needed that so much.
I'm so glad I camped out from 5pm on Friday for the Saturday concert because it meant I managed to get to the barrier just off centre, being that close to the people who saved my life and gave me a future without even knowing it was just...well words can't do it justice.
Without My Chemical Romance I would be dead, they kept me alive. Seeing them perform was the first time in my life that I actually started to heal and recover from my past. I'm autistic and become fixated and obsessed with certain things, my two main ones are horses and My Chemical Romance. They are the very core of my being; I physically couldn't function without them. Nobody will ever really understand just how much they mean to me because I need them just as much as I need oxygen."
Tegan Longcroft (Cambridge, UK)

"I saw them for the first-time last night after loving them since 2007 when I was aged 11/12.
*I cried to '**Helena**' and '**Black Parade**' because those songs got me through so much as a teenager and hearing them live made me realise, I might not be who I am today, or even still here if it wasn't for MCR.*
I've had a rough 2022 and seeing them live made me feel alive again."
Chloe Jackson (Leeds, UK)

The Fans Have Their Say #15 My Chemical Romance

"I'm 53 and first saw them in 2011 when I took my eldest daughter who was 15 at the time. Been hooked ever since.
This time I went with my youngest 2 daughters and their friend.
It's been a long time coming but was so worth the wait and a broken foot to boot." **Wendy Ahmed (UK)**

"I've been a fan since 2003/2004 I found MCR at a time in my life where everything else was turned upside down. I was a young girl in a highly abusive and negligent household with music being my only escape, I would put my headphones in on my Walkman and everything else would melt away.
Almost like it gave me the strength to just carry on.
Things got better after I left that environment, but I had to start my life over, knowing no one. I met my best friend through our mutual love of MCR and I declared she was my new favourite person.
That was 16 years ago, when we were younger and heard that the band split and needed to stop for their own health and wellbeing we were absolutely gutted, being from a working-class area I didn't even ask if I could go to their gigs as I knew we were too poor to afford things like that; it was just one of them things.
I resigned myself to the fact I'd never experience their music live in front of me.
16 years on and my friend and I - a little bit older with a few more kids between us - finally got to stand next to each other and belt out **'Headfirst for Halos'** *I had her pinch my arm because, I couldn't believe this was actually happening.*
I really cannot say how my life would've panned out without MCR influencing me. Maybe I wouldn't even be here. I definitely wouldn't have the chosen family and support system I do now, my child wouldn't have her favourite auntie.
This band helped me stay alive at a time I didn't really know how to be, and then gave me a family I'd never had before through it, so in recognition of that I got myself this tattoo to represent a big part of my life. The experience the build up everything was amazing.
It was worth the wait.
I don't think I'll be leaving it as long to see them next time, though!"
Alee Bampton (UK)

The Fans Have Their Say #15 My Chemical Romance

The Fans Have Their Say #15 My Chemical Romance

"The 19th May was an out of body experience for me!
It was my first ever gig - as I am autistic - and I was on my own.
So many emotions soared through me as the boys were playing some of the songs that have literally saved my life. I felt this at peace feeling at the end of the concert and it seemed that all my anger and sadness that I'd had to bottle up over the weeks before had somehow been pulled out by the boys during the set.
Gerard going on a tangent about his cat in the bloodied suit was just what I'd heard about previous concerts, and it was just what I'd dreamed it would be. Although it was my first gig, I got this sense of coming home with every song played.
It was the experience of a lifetime, and I loved every second of it!"
Jessica Littleton (UK)

"After a very uncertain 2'ish years, where I genuinely thought these shows wouldn't go on, my friend and I were finally able to see the band we'd loved since we were teens. Both in our early 30's, we reminisced about the fandom and the memories we had from years ago.
But being in that show on the 21st of May 2022 was like I was 15 again.
As soon as the smoke machine came on, and the weird static buzzing became a clear indicator that the show was starting, I was holding back the tears. It had been so long, and I was just overcome with relief and happiness. It was happening, and my heroes were taking to the stage.
The band were incredible as always, the set list was amazing (they played one of my all-time favourites '**Bulletproof Heart**' and I may have injured my throat from screaming along Haha) and it was just an amazing night!
The fans were excited, you could feel the energy from everyone around you. I just wanted to keep singing and cheering all night long.
When they played '**Famous Last Words**' and the bridge started, everyone was singing along, and I got chills. The fandom was in unison. We'd all waited so long, and we were all there, singing along to such powerful lyrics. It was an amazing experience.
Gerard has always been an incredible front man and this show was no exception. He lights up the stage and commands everyone's attention. Frank was a bundle of excitement, but when the crowd got too much, he became a voice of reason and was able to guide everyone safely back quickly. It was so so nice to see Mikey and Ray so happy too, playing with such passion and energy.
When the band left the stage and the show had ended, I felt happy that I had been able to experience this once again, but sad that it was over. I certainly won't be forgetting that show anytime soon.

The Fans Have Their Say #15 My Chemical Romance

I always say to people that MCR know how to put on an amazing show and in my eyes they never disappoint. I eagerly await whatever the band decide to do next (as long as it's not breaking up again ha-ha)."
Dani Panic (UK)

MK Stadium, Milton Keynes, UK 21st May 2022

The Foundations of Decay
I'm Not Okay (I Promise)
Give 'Em Hell Kid
Make Room!!!
Summertime
Bulletproof Heart
This Is How I Disappear
You Know What They Do to Guys Like Us in Prison
Na Na Na (Na Na Na Na Na Na Na Na Na)
Famous Last Words
Surrender the Night
Teenagers
DESTROYA
Our Lady of Sorrows
Vampire Money
Thank You for the Venom
Mama
Welcome to the Black Parade
Sleep
Boy Division
Helena

The Fans Have Their Say #15 My Chemical Romance

*"I went to their MK gig on the 21st of May with my 2 close friends and my sister. I have been listening to them since '**Bullets...**' was released in 2002 and it was worth the wait after having bought these tickets on their release date.*
I have struggled with addiction for many years, and recently celebrated 1 year clean. I was able to listen to Gerard's singing completely sober, and it was such a beautiful experience.
*When they played their last song, '**Helena**', I became so overwhelmed by what I've accomplished in this last year that I burst into tears.*
I hope that I can one day thank Gerard, Mikey, Ray and Frank for unknowingly sharing those moments with me, I will never forget them."
Chloé (UK)

*"My favourite moment from MK on 19th, standing in a sea of fans singing '**Ghost of You**' at the top of our lungs with tears destroying my eyeliner and thinking I've been waiting so long for this moment and it's perfect."*
Zoe Pryce (Airdrie, North Lanarkshire, Scotland, UK)

"Longest wait for me for a concert but was worth it for the amazing atmosphere!"
Colin Osmond-Wright (Bushbury, Wolverhampton, UK)

"So glad I went to see them at the NEC in Birmingham.
The visit to Milton Keynes was a total rip off. I've learned not to go to football stadiums for a gig if you're in seated. The screens were useless. They sounded like they had been inhaling helium. Never again."
Nuala McNaught (UK)

"Well, it finally happened, only 2 years of waiting, a fantastic night.
*The guys were flawless as ever; Gerard getting thoughtful, Frank going into Dad mode, Mikey actually getting his 'Fucking Ready' at the beginning of '**Vampire Money**' and Ray just being Ray, constantly grinning and running around like a five-year-old.*
Jellybeans first gig, she had a fantastic time, I think I might have set the bar a bit high there, oh well, let's see how she fares with Green Day next month. Expecting Aaron to be almost mute for a few days, now to get my hearing back, you know what they say, if you can still hear and speak at the end of a concert, you're not doing it right, if it's too loud you're too old."
Caz Berry (Dartford, UK)

The Fans Have Their Say #15 My Chemical Romance

"I started listening to MCR about 15 years ago now!
In 2014 at the age of 15, I got to see G perform '**Hesitant Alien**' in Cardiff with my mama Esta Lippiatt who is also a huge fan! I had just recovered from surgery in February and saw him November 9th, 2014, G was brilliant, and the fans were also so careful and kind! It was a once in a lifetime experience, but I never ever thought my dream of seeing the whole band would come true, it honestly felt impossible!
 I can't explain how happy, excited and truly grateful I am for what they've done and put together for all us Killjoys!
The 17th of May 2022 at the Eden project was the most insanely amazing experience I've ever had, the band are absolutely fantastic on stage, their chemistry together is adorable, and the performance is something no other band could top in my opinion! The sass is alive as my mama said! All the merch is awesome, I love my beanie, I'll treasure it forever!
Also, a special shout out to the security at the concert who really helped my mum and I, they got us into the quiet area as they could see we were struggling with our disabilities! All in all, the perfect night."
Kymberley Watson-Lippiatt (Camborne, Cornwall, UK)

"Thanks to my daughter Kymberley for playing MCR in the car, back on our morning school runs (2012) I started really loving the music at that time - probably a bit later than some ppl - but I've been a massive fan since then.
I couldn't believe when they announced their split in 2013 & nearly cried like a teenager, like when Kurt Cobain passed!
We went to see Gerard in 2014 & omg, I felt alive again!
It's been way too quiet after that, although I have listened to MCR or G every day since then. When my daughter texted me to tell me about

The Fans Have Their Say #15 My Chemical Romance

'*Foundations of Decay*' - OMG! Tears of joy & have been listening to it on repeat... it may be one of the best songs they've written!
I never thought I'd actually get to see the whole band together again but Tuesday May 17th, 2022, at Eden, near where we live, all my dreams came true!
45 years old & screaming like a teenage girl yet again. Best experience of my life apart from having my children!
So, thanks to my daughter for encouraging me to listen & more thanks to the guys of MCR who have got me through some very dark times.
You are incredible human beings."
Esta Lippiatt (Camborne, Cornwall, UK)

"My chemical romance always had my back, I got into them at 11 years old and they got me through so much. They got me through being groomed and abused, they got me through being bullied, they got me through suffering from bpd. They told me it was okay to not be okay and made me feel less alone in this world. Music bonded me and so many of my best friends together - I even met one during the MCRmy meetups back in the day.
The night before the gig, we had a sleepover-watched "the black parade is dead" together whilst sobbing, then all got dressed and painted up in our old emo warpaint.
A group of us all got up super early on the morning of the gig and queued up all day.
We got pretty close to the front, holding hands as we filled with suspense waiting for the show to begin.
As "the foundations of decay" started to play, I felt a glow of euphoria and an overwhelming amount of emotion. Throughout the whole gig we

The Fans Have Their Say #15 My Chemical Romance

kept grabbing each other with excitement and screaming how we can't believe it was real.

Then the peak moment hit. They started to play cemetery drive - my favourite song that had got me through many depressions in my life. My friends through this number lifted me above their heads, it felt as if my chemical romance were singing and looking specifically at me. It was genuinely one of the most incredible moments of my life. As the show went on, the setlist stayed incredible with them playing cancer and headfirst for halos - both leaving me an emotional mess. It was one of the best nights of my life and worth the unbelievably long wait. To complete this amazing experience my partner is taking me to see the European shows after this. After going through hell for the longest time, I can't believe my chemical romance are back and they are supporting me through the amazing times and the healthy relationships I never dreamed I would ever have."

Charlie Hope (London)

"So..., where to begin. I probably need to give some context/background of why they are so important to me first.

I suppose I would be deemed as an 'elder Emo' having been a fan from their first album which was released when I was 14. I was the outcast at school, the nerd, the geek, the easy target and whilst I loved school, I hated my classmates. My Chem were the band I found that I could stick on and listen to that I related to. Homelife wasn't much better with a bitter separation taking place between parents which often became violent.

In 2005 I lost my older brother to suicide and again I found myself turning to My Chem, particularly '**Ghost of You**' which was released mere weeks after it happened. Grieving alongside my favourite band willed me to go on and I found myself at university in 2006 studying music.

'**The Black Parade**' blew up and '**Famous Last Words**' became my anthem, after my own struggles with depression.

When the opportunity came up to see them, I roped in friends to make sure I bagged myself a ticket. I'd never had the chance to see them before due to money, family, life stuff so, short of selling a kidney I would have done most anything to make sure I was there. The gig was everything I hoped it to be and more. They have travelled with me through my life for 20 years, been with me in all my successes (Cue: '**Sing**'), my break ups (Cue: '**I Don't Love You**'), my failures (Cue: '**I'm Not Okay (I Promise)**'), and my fuck it moments (Cue: '**I Never Told You What I Do For a Living**').

Their energy onstage and the way they interact with us as family. I spent a lot of the gig either screaming the words along or in tears of joy (and occasionally sadness when they played '**Ghost of You**').

The white flag moment was so moving too. Such a beautiful way to remember those we've lost along the way.

The gig was over before it had even started it felt like. One the highlights of my life was to finally see My Chem after a lifetime of them willing me to 'Carry on'."

Emma Cooper (UK)

MK Stadium, Milton Keynes, UK 22nd May 2022

The Foundations of Decay
Na Na Na (Na Na Na Na Na Na Na Na Na)
Give 'Em Hell Kid
Mastas of Ravencroft
Cemetery Drive
Helena
Boy Division
House of Wolves
Welcome to the Black Parade
Teenagers
The Ghost of You
DESTROYA
The Only Hope for Me Is You
Vampire Money
Thank You for the Venom
Mama
S/C/A/R/E/C/R/O/W
Famous Last Words
Cancer
Headfirst for Halos
I'm Not Okay (I Promise)

"*I am 55 yrs. old, and my daughter is 16 yrs. old, we both love MCR.*

The Fans Have Their Say #15 My Chemical Romance

We saw them at Eden on their first night of the tour. They were awesome and the atmosphere was truly amazing.
I was delighted they played **'The Foundations of Decay'** *first it is a brilliant song and means a lot to me already.*
My daughter sobbed at the end of the concert with happiness because their music has helped her through some very difficult times.
They will always be a very special band to us."
Mandi Osborne (St. Austell, Cornwall, UK)

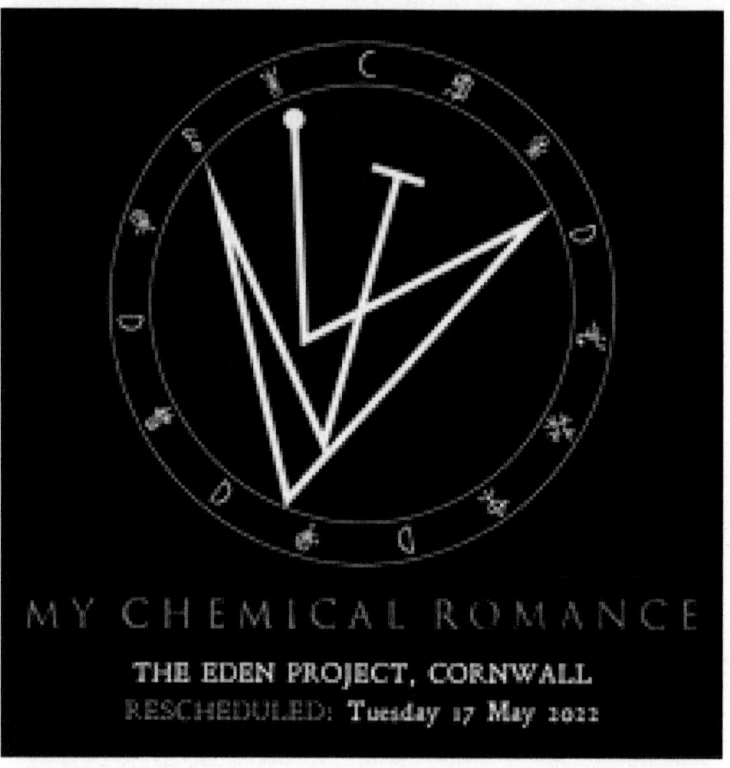

"*I followed them from the start, being an alternative band, it was not something my friends were into, but I loved them their energy and everything about them.*
But Gerard well what I can I say?
He has the most beautiful face of any male person put on earth; it was truly love at first sight.
I became a single mum. As the years passed, I listened alone to their music then **'The Black Parade'** *came out and was put in the charts so everyone accepted MCR, but for me it was the norm, I always loved them.*

The Fans Have Their Say #15 My Chemical Romance

Anyway, 2013 came, the band split and I carried on listening and always will do I followed them on Instagram and Twitter, then always knew what they were up too.

2019 came, my boys were back! Tickets released then boom the pandemic. Unfortunately, I didn't get a ticket. I was devastated. Then all of a sudden more tickets were released so I got one for the 16th of May Eden show. Took my mate who liked them but wasn't really a fan and my 15 yr. old son and wow what can I say they blew me away phenomenal.

I'm so in love with the band, even more now, but that wasn't enough, so I struggled but I got two more tickets for me and my 15 yr. old and we're seeing them again on Saturday 28th May at Cardiff, Wales; were from Cornwall so driving up and staying the night in Bristol.

*So anyway, that's a bit about me. My older children's dad passed away June 5th, 2021, suddenly - he had the look of Gerard, bless his heart and will be truly missed. We were very good friends and once again MCR got me through it. Also, my mum passed away on 18th January 2016 so as much as I love the song I always cry when I hear '**Cancer**' as that was how she died.*

My lifelong dream is to be signed by the band, for me to get it tattooed."
Paula Nicholls (Cornwall, UK)

"*As an elder Emo, one of the things that stood out to me at the MK 21.05 gig was the amount of baby Emo's there was. I found it was so heart-warming knowing that there was a new generation of Emo's to carry on loving a band that I have loved since I was their ages.*

Another thing that stuck out to me and made me thankful for being part of the fandom, was seeing all the outfits everyone had chosen. Everyone looked so different and unique but at the same time so recognisable as a MCR fan. There were fans that wore the same shirts, but their overall looks were so different but equally as perfect.

The atmosphere within the gig was unique and showed a great sense of togetherness."
Natashia Murden (UK)

"*I wouldn't be here without MCR.*
The first time around, when I was very young suffering with horrendous mental health, and once again they've helped me get through things now. Parts of life have taken another nosedive and I will keep pushing on now I've seen them. It makes me remember why I get up and try to have some sort of normal life everyday now being disabled.
They are worth their weight - and so much more - in gold."
Emma Walbridge (UK)

The Fans Have Their Say #15 My Chemical Romance

"I've been a fan since 2006. I was 13 when '**Welcome to the Black Parade**' was released and I vividly remember hearing it on a music channel playing on the TV and running over to see what this sound was. I was hooked.
I then spent the next 16 years trying to learn as much as I could about the band and their music. I was offered a ticket to go and see them perform in Plymouth for '**the Black Parade**' tour by someone at my school, but my social anxiety stopped me and when they later went on hiatus, I genuinely thought I had missed the chance to ever see them live.
Fast forward and they release a comeback tour.
On the day the MK tickets were released, we crashed 3 computers at work trying to get me on and get tickets. We managed it and I later also bought tickets to see them at the Eden Project and Cardiff. As I write this, I've been to two of these gigs, with Cardiff happening next weekend.
I've never felt like I truly belonged in a group of people. Don't get me wrong, I'm lucky to have a large group of fantastic friends but I always felt a bit different. A bit weird. Always the weirdest in a group. But not at one of their gigs. I finally felt like I belonged. Like I was with my people. Not the weirdest person, just another member of the family. Everyone I've met so far has been so friendly and supportive.
When the band came out onto the stage at the Eden Project, I was moved to tears because I still couldn't believe this was actually happening and my heart was so full of love for all of them. I love Gerrard's chat, Mikey's incredible presence, Frank's cheekiness and seeing Ray just having the best time headbanging and dancing around. The best bit is watching them having a genuinely great time with each other.
They're not just a band to me. They're almost more than family, they feel like a part of me, almost like musical soul mates. Their music has been with me during the worst and best days and I'm still working out how to include them in my wedding, which is less than 2 months away!
If I could say one thing to the lads, it would simply be 'thank you'."
Kt English (UK)

"I remember having MCR playing in the car when my kids were little. 2 little voices in the back belting out '**Black Parade…**' (aged about 3 & 4). As they got older my daughter rediscovered them for herself and I'm pretty sure they've saved her life a couple of times. It's been a rough few years for her depression.
Watching her sing on Saturday night and lose herself to the music was the best feeling in the world.
MCR brought my baby back."
Jo Newington (UK)

The Fans Have Their Say #15 My Chemical Romance

"I've never been a fan of My Chemical Romance, I took my daughter to watch them perform last night (22/05/22) as she is a massive fan, and it was our first ever concert... All I can say is WOW! Their performance was spot on and full of energy, to top it off the atmosphere of the crowd was beyond amazing!
Extremely pleased we went and if we had another chance, yes, I would go and see them perform again."
Natashya Meldrum (Newhaven, East Sussex, UK)

"Longest wait for me for a concert but was worth it for the amazing atmosphere!" **Colin Osmond-Wright (Bushbury, Wolverhampton, UK)**

*"I started listening to MCR CD '****The Black Parade****' on the back hand of me listening to 30 seconds to Mars, and I'm not sure how now, but I was going through a real rough time. I had 4 kids at the time and needed something to connect with. And I did.*
But I missed out on them as I was a young mum, so never really went to concerts partying.
But when I split from my boyfriend in 2011, I found them and still to this day I love them. My family don't get it.

The Fans Have Their Say #15 My Chemical Romance

The songs sound depressing or weird they say. But to me they lift me up and I connect. I wear black clothes because I like black, they don't get it. I'm not all out there. But I do not fit in very well anywhere. And I get a lot of comfort in these songs along with all kinds of music.
But I have these cd's in my car every day and back up cos for when they break lol. The car is my stage where either can blast them and sing along.

The concert I travelled alone and came alone. But when they came on, I was full of happiness. I'm so happy I got to see the theatrical Gerard dressed up, that was awesome and not expected at all.
A strange unrelated connection my daughter says rats randomly and when he stood there and said rats it was like it was meant to be heard lol, I am a little gutted we couldn't stand there and have all the greats playing but time waits for no one. Just hoping they come around again for a bigger better longer set. And I will be there.
I never thought I could use my ticket due to covid restrictions and so when they were dropped, I had a whole lot of 'I got a ticket' excitement all over again.
Thank you MCR. And I love the new song."
Tegan Murrell (UK)

"So where to start about MCR!
When I first heard them back in 2003, I was 11 and was like this band have a cool vibe but then I was still into N-Sync etc! Then I started High School and I listened to them a bit more and discovered my identity, I was only 13 at the time, pleaded with my mum to take me a show but because it wasn't her kind of music she refused.
Ages 14-17 I dealt with some pretty rough times in my life some good, some bad but MCR were the only band that I turned my attentions back to, just listening to the songs and the words made me just 'CARRY ON', then they split up just as I was given freedom to go to concerts on my own, so here I was longing to see a band that has meant so much to me but also grieving for the loss of possibly never being able to see them perform live!
*I discovered my love for '**Helena**', making it now my number 1 favorite MCR song of all time, the words, the music video I'm just completely obsessed with!*
Fast forward to 2020, I'd just lost my grandfather and I listened to MCR more than ever, I found a post about MCR doing a UK Tour and I thought nah this can't be true, then the tickets went up for sale and the first 2 lots sold within minutes, when I tell you I was devastated - like I ugly cried for days!

The Fans Have Their Say #15 My Chemical Romance

Then I met my soulmate and discovered he liked MCR too, so with the help of him, my mum and every device we all owned, when the 3rd lot of tickets was released, I finally managed to get my hands on 2 tickets, and I was so pumped! But then of course covid threw a spanner in the works and postponed the concert twice making it seem like I was never going to see them live...

I nearly got my tickets refunded, I was just heartbroken, so this was like now or never 2022!

So, here I was the week starting 15.05.2022 and the nerves were literally kicking in. My anxiety was at an all-time high, 4 days until I see MCR...I was counting down the days!

18.05.2022 - I arrive with my partner and check into the Hilton Hotel attached to the Stadium, we were greeted with a cookie and then we heard soundcheck, we sneaked a peek at Sound check, and I saw Gerard on stage and my little heart was like OMG OMG OMG!

The morning of the 19.05.2022 came around so quick and I was ready, up, showered the lot before 8am. Me and my partner walked around to Gate 5 which was closest to the stage and got in queue, we were number 53&54. I was so calm throughout the whole queuing process, talking to all the amazing fans, seeing everyone so excited for the concert they'd been anticipating for 2 years...

2pm and they started handing the wristbands out 'FRONT PIT' was written on it, and I squealed I was like

'HOLY COW I'M GOING TO BE NEAR THE FRONT'.

3pm came and the panic was starting to set in. I felt clammy and sick with excitement, but my partner calmed me down. I had a few minor panic moments in the stadium as well, but everyone was so lovely and calming! Then they came on stage, and I just burst into tears and had the best time. Sobbed during '*Helena*' of course and then my partner got me to barrier because I was being squashed and I saw everything!

It was honestly a dream come true and I'd do it all again in a heartbeat."
Laura Ann (Braintree, Essex, UK)

"After waiting 2years for this - it was so worth the wait; unfortunately, I was a member down in our group but still had an amazing time."
Lauz Dear (Eastleigh, UK)

"I'm 58 and they got me through the lockdown!

I liked them when they were first around but not with any sort of passion and then I listened to '*the Black Parade*' album, and it went from there.

I started collecting everything, Gerard and his comics and listened to all the music and hunted down collectables and discovered the community

The Fans Have Their Say #15 My Chemical Romance

which all came together for the comeback, and I was honoured to be a part of it. Outstanding!
And my daughter and I have memories we will cherish forever."
Linda Dollin (Fleetwood, UK)

"I've been a fan for just over a year now and tonight 22nd May I had experienced my first ever concert with MCR and it has and will be the best show I've seen, and I will carry it on."
Caitlin Meldrum Lavallee (Newhaven, East Sussex, UK)

"I am 30 and I have been listening to MCR since I was 15 and I see them for the 1st time on Thursday 19th May, and I was amazed by the band I felt like a teenager again. It was amazing to hear some songs from the 1st album and to hear '*I'm Not OK...*' live was amazing and I can't wait to see if they tour again."
Harley Moffat (Stanford Le Hope, UK)

"Me and my best friend (Lauren) have always loved My Chemical Romance and we finally got to see them at MK!
19th of May 2022 is one of the best days of our lives getting to see them live. Lots of laughter and tears were shared during the concert of a lifetime.
My Chemical Romance has got me through a lot in life and I am so thankful for them.
The crowd was absolutely amazing, and everyone was so nice. It will never be forgotten."
Mary Middleton (Milton Keynes, UK)

The Fans Have Their Say #15 My Chemical Romance

"My mum, my son and I came Saturday, I have been a massive fan since MCR first came out!

I'm now 35 and still love them and their music! And my son got to see them on his 13th birthday! And that is the age I was when I first heard them!!!

And my mum would listen over and over and write down all the lyrics for me!

I was 13 when I first discovered MCR and on Saturday when we saw them my son turned 13 and I remember exactly how I felt at that age! and all 3 of us saw them for the first time! What an amazing experience!!

My Chemical Romance Saved My Life!!!

They were fantastic! I wish I was able to see them more than once on this tour, but so grateful for being able to see them at all.

G seemed so happy."

Natasha Harris (Guildford, UK)

"We went to see MCR twice. 19th May was for my early 30th present. And then I got free tickets for the 21st.

And OMG it was amazing.

Me and my partner loved every minute of. He doesn't really like this kind of music, but he liked the music and the atmosphere and love in the concerts. I loved it so much and I want to see them again!!!

Never spending 2 hours in the merch queue again though".

Zelinaa Simone (UK)

The Fans Have Their Say #15 My Chemical Romance

The Fans Have Their Say #15 My Chemical Romance

Royal Hospital Kilmainham, Dublin, Ireland 24th May 2022

The Foundations of Decay
I'm Not Okay (I Promise)
Give 'Em Hell Kid
Tomorrow's Money
Summertime
The Only Hope for Me Is You
Boy Division
House of Wolves
Na Na Na (Na Na Na Na Na Na Na Na Na)
It's Not a Fashion Statement, It's a Fucking Deathwish
Teenagers
The Ghost of You
DESTROYA
Welcome to the Black Parade
Vampire Money
Mama
Famous Last Words
Skylines and Turnstiles
Helena

The Fans Have Their Say #15 My Chemical Romance

At Eden Sessions 17th May 2022

The Fans Have Their Say #15 My Chemical Romance

Royal Hospital Kilmainham, Dublin, Ireland 25th May 2022

The Foundations of Decay
DESTROYA
Thank You For the Venom
Bulletproof Heart
This Is How I Disappear
You Know What They Do to Guys Like Us in Prison
Na Na Na (Na Na Na Na Na Na Na Na Na)
Famous Last Words
Surrender the Night
Teenagers
Helena
Our Lady of Sorrows
Vampire Money
Make Room!!!!
Mama
Welcome to the Black Parade
Sleep
I'm Not Okay (I Promise)
The Kids From Yesterday

The Fans Have Their Say #15 My Chemical Romance

"I was at the MCR show in Dublin on May 24, 2022. What an INCREDIBLE experience! The venue at Royal Hospital Kilmainham was breath-taking & fit My Chem's vibe so well. The guards were funny & kind, and I had a blast interacting with other fans throughout the evening.

I was in the pit, about three rows from the barrier on the right side of the stage (in front of Ray). It was my first MCR show, and I was having the time of my life singing along to every word, chatting with other fans, laughing at Gerard's asides, & dancing the night away.

Here are a few highlights from the evening:

- the security guard at bag check asking if we brought alcohol and then sounding disappointed when we said no.

- Gerard's voice giving out & him then making indistinguishable Batman/Gollum/Stitch noises. He also talked about how the band was having so much fun on this tour & how he didn't care about how his voice sounded anymore.

- the crowd chanting "f*ck the Queen!" when Gerard mentioned the idea of performing for the Queen and then realized he was in the Irish Republic and not in the UK

- Gerard talking about duct tape, his Eddie Vedder journal, & complaining about having to drink canned seltzer water because it was hard to find regular (non-sparkling) water in Ireland.

- MCR playing **'Tomorrow's Money'** *live for the FIRST time.*

Fun fact, after the show, a bunch of people - including myself - crowded around the merch stand in hopes they would open it back up (the venue apparently only allowed one merch stand). Somehow, I ended up at the very back of the line and waited for probably an hour and a half-long after the venue was supposed to be closed - before I was finally able to get helped. Turns out I was the VERY LAST person left in the venue (aside from staff) and I had to be personally escorted out by security.

Everyone was lovely, though, and I wouldn't trade the experience for anything."
Christa Wilson (Sherwood, AR, USA)

The Fans Have Their Say #15 My Chemical Romance

CHRISTA WILSON

"I went to the Cardiff event it was insane.
From queuing up and meeting people, everyone got along.
The concert was amazing from the openers to the main show, the screaming when they arrived on stage plays in my mind on repeat (as well as the g note) but being 2 rows from the barrier made it even better.
Being able to scream/sing and just have the most amazing time it definitely was worth it and definitely is something I can never forget."
Torie Williams (Pontypool, Wales, UK)

"Me and my partner were at the gig 19th May at MK, and we had to book last minute tickets to go back for the Sunday 22nd gig too.
Going both times felt like coming home.
Everyone in the audience were so amazingly supportive of each other. You could talk to a stranger like you were old friends catching up. You could be yourself with no shame or judgement. It was easily best thing I've ever experienced. One thing Gerard said on stage that resonated so much with me (on the Sunday show) was "this is living... This is what living feels like" and it's true, being in that audience was the most alive I've ever felt."
Diana Williams (London, UK)

The Fans Have Their Say #15 My Chemical Romance

"My daughter Ebony is a huge MCR fan, her favourite band for many years.
She finally got the chance to see them play at Victoria Park Warrington and had the best time ever, also my first MCR gig and I loved them...
The crowd were amazing everyone so happy and looking after each other.

This is a pic of us in the VIP area.
Just to add that at our Warrington gig it was really funny when Gerrard addressed the crowd as Manchester, he then realised that he was in Warrington or maybe someone reminded him! I think he completely forgot because he had stayed in a Manchester hotel and thought he was still in Manchester!
He was spotted at the Lowrey Hotel, I just thought it was really funny and it made me giggle."

Alexandria Meadows (Manchester, UK)

The Fans Have Their Say #15 My Chemical Romance

Victoria Park, Warrington, UK 27th May 2022

The Foundations of Decay
Na Na Na (Na Na Na Na Na Na Na Na Na)
Give 'Em Hell Kid
Tomorrow's Money
Thank You For the Venom
The Only Hope For Me Is You
Boy Division
House of Wolves
Welcome to the Black Parade
Teenagers
The Ghost of You
DESTROYA
Summertime
Vampire Money
Helena
Mama
S/C/A/R/E/C/R/O/W
Famous Last Words
Cancer
Mastas of Ravenkroft
I'm Not Okay (I Promise)

The Fans Have Their Say #15 My Chemical Romance

*"We were at MK on the 19th of May 2022.
This was supposed to be for Jo's 40th birthday but the pandemic saw the dates put back twice, she turned 42 yesterday.
We had the time of our lives…"*
Jon Bage (UK)

The Fans Have Their Say #15 My Chemical Romance

"I had discovered MCR shortly before the breakup, so I never thought I'd see them play live. The overwhelming joy when the announcement of the reunion came was indescribable, and when I actually got tickets for Rotterdam in January 2020 I was over the moon.
We all know what happened next...
So, when the show eventually took place, I felt my heart was about to burst. It was one of the best nights in my life, so filled with emotion that I had to cry a few times. Me, a 56-year-old woman, sobbing like a teenager. I don't have one special moment; the whole evening was magical. Thank you for the music, for the love and the joy."
Inge Luijendijk-Vijgen (Brielle, Netherlands)

The Fans Have Their Say #15 My Chemical Romance

Sophia Gardens Cricket Ground, Cardiff, UK 28th May 2022

The Foundations of Decay
Thank You For the Venom
Bulletproof Heart
This Is How I Disappear
You Know What They Do to Guys Like Us in Prison
Na Na Na (Na Na Na Na Na Na Na Na Na)
Famous Last Words
Save Yourself, I'll Hold Them Back
DESTROYA
Teenagers
Helena
Our Lady of Sorrows
Vampire Money
Mama
Welcome to the Black Parade
Sleep
I'm Not Okay (I Promise)

The Fans Have Their Say #15 My Chemical Romance

"I went to Milton Keynes on the 19th (the 10th anniversary of their last show) and Warrington on the 27th.
As long-time sufferer of anxiety and depression, this band's music has helped get me through so much of it, I don't know where I'd be otherwise. So finally, being able to see them live for the first time, especially after almost resigning myself to the idea that it was a near impossible wish, was something I had to do when given the chance.
 It was such an incredible experience, hearing some of the songs that kept me going, it was as emotional as it gets.
It was an experience that I will never forget.
I also got to meet some amazing people in the VIP line, at the front row barrier, and on the train home to Liverpool too."
Paul McGowan (Liverpool, UK)

"After waiting for the Covid-19 pandemic to come to an end, would the show be worth it? Of course, it would.
Attending the second Eden Sessions date in Cornwall was a little bit of a letdown though, for two reasons –

1) It was originally set to be the first UK for MCR since they reformed.
2) The first date - the day before – they added the amazing Frank Turner as support!

It was annoying, but the show more than made up for it! Now they need to headline Reading & Leeds or Download Festival in 2023!"
Ian Carroll (Plymouth, UK)

The Fans Have Their Say #15 My Chemical Romance

"I've listened to My Chemical Romance for many years being of the slightly older generation than my youngest daughter who saw them in Milton Keynes in May.

The build-up in the stadium was phenomenal and when they came on and Gerard started singing their latest song, I am not ashamed to say I stood there and cried happy tears!!

To actually see them in the flesh after years of listening to their songs it is a memory I will never forget."

Andrea Goodwin (Doncaster, UK)

The Fans Have Their Say #15 My Chemical Romance

PAUL MCGOWAN
WARRINGTON

Backstage at Reading Festival

The Fans Have Their Say #15 My Chemical Romance

"I've basically waited half of my life to see MCR again in Rotterdam last week. I saw them 14 years ago in my home country.
When they broke up in 2013, I was devastated and thought I would never see them together again. But alas, the future is kind enough to let me see them in flesh once more.
Emotions welled up as soon as they started playing, and my inner teenage self was brought back to life. When they sang **'Famous Last Words'***, I cried so much because it became my life anthem when they disbanded (temporarily).*
It felt surreal seeing them again after a long time.
MCR shaped my personality, and I wouldn't be what I am now if not for them. Heck, I even got a degree in journalism so I can interview them someday! Haha."
Sara Bee (Ermelo, Netherlands)

"I've been a fan since 2009 and finally after 13 years I had the pleasure and the honour to attend the show on MK the 22 of May.
It was the best night of my life.
The atmosphere was amazing, the whole crowd chanting the songs it filled my heart with happy tears and joy.
The guys were AMAZING I'll never forget those memories. MCR helped me a lot during my life being one of the loners, bullied and left out kids and they keep saving me every day. They even brought me my best friend Frankie Cobaugh. I love this community so much, nobody judges you, everyone cares for each other cause we all share similar stories, and this is the best sensation in the world "Being heard, being understood"."
Lea Taravella (Palermo, Italy)

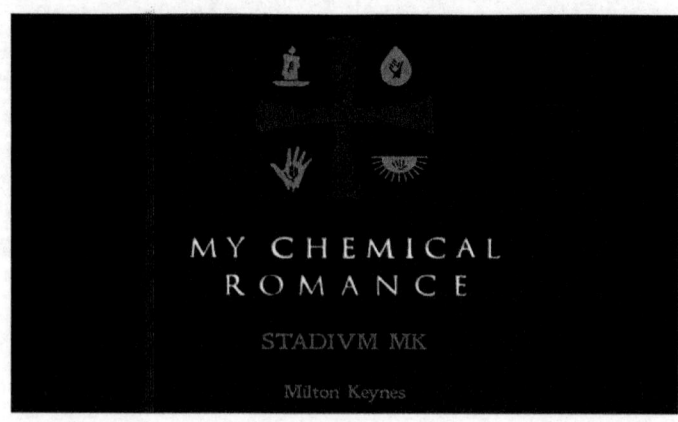

The Fans Have Their Say #15 My Chemical Romance

The OVO, Glasgow, UK 28th May 2022

The Foundations of Decay
Helena
Give 'Em Hell Kid
Male Room!!!!
Summertime
The Only Hope for Me Is You
Boy Division
You Know What They Do to Guys Like Us in Prison
Na Na Na (Na Na Na Na Na Na Na Na Na)
Famous Last Words
Surrender the Night
Teenagers
Save Yourself, I'll Hold Them Back
DESTROYA
Our Lady of Sorrows
Vampire Money
Thank You For the Venom
Mama
Welcome to the Black Parade
Sleep
I'm Not Okay (I Promise)

The Fans Have Their Say #15 My Chemical Romance

The Fans Have Their Say #15 My Chemical Romance

Eden Sessions – 2nd Date 17th May 2022

The Fans Have Their Say #15 My Chemical Romance

The Fans Have Their Say #15 My Chemical Romance

MY CHEMICAL ROMANCE

FOUNDATIONS
HELENA
GIVE EM HELL
MAKE ROOM
SUMMERTIME

DISAPPEAR
PRISON
NANANA
FAMOUS
SURRENDER
TEENAGERS
I DON'T LOVE YOU
DESTROYA
SORROWS
VAMPIRE $$
VENOM
MAMA
BLACK PARADE
SLEEP

BOY DIVISION
NOT OK
KIDS

A

EDEN PROJECT MAY 16TH 2022

The Fans Have Their Say #15 My Chemical Romance

Upcoming Festival Dates

The Fans Have Their Say #15 My Chemical Romance

The Fans Have Their Say #15 My Chemical Romance

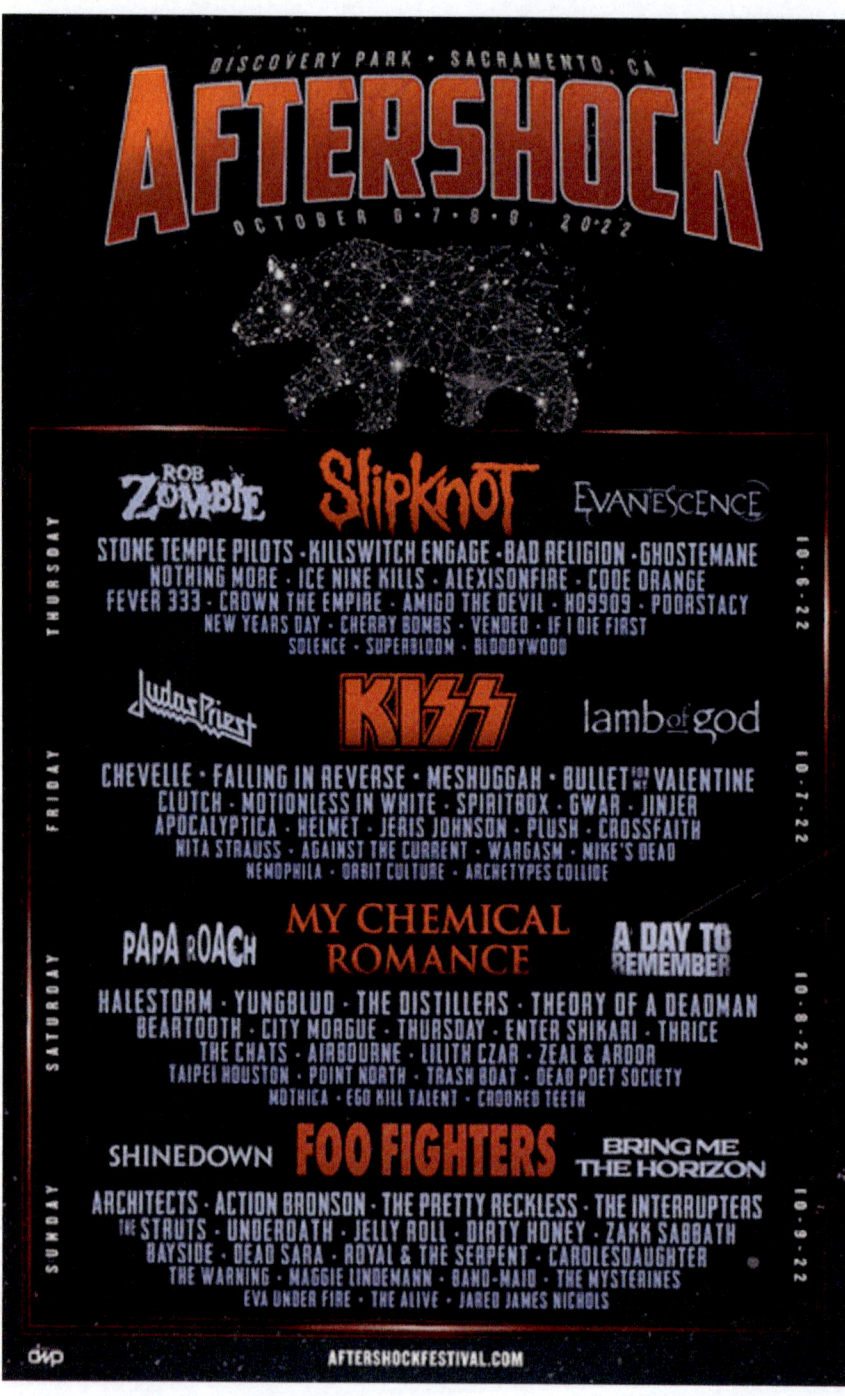

The Fans Have Their Say #15 My Chemical Romance

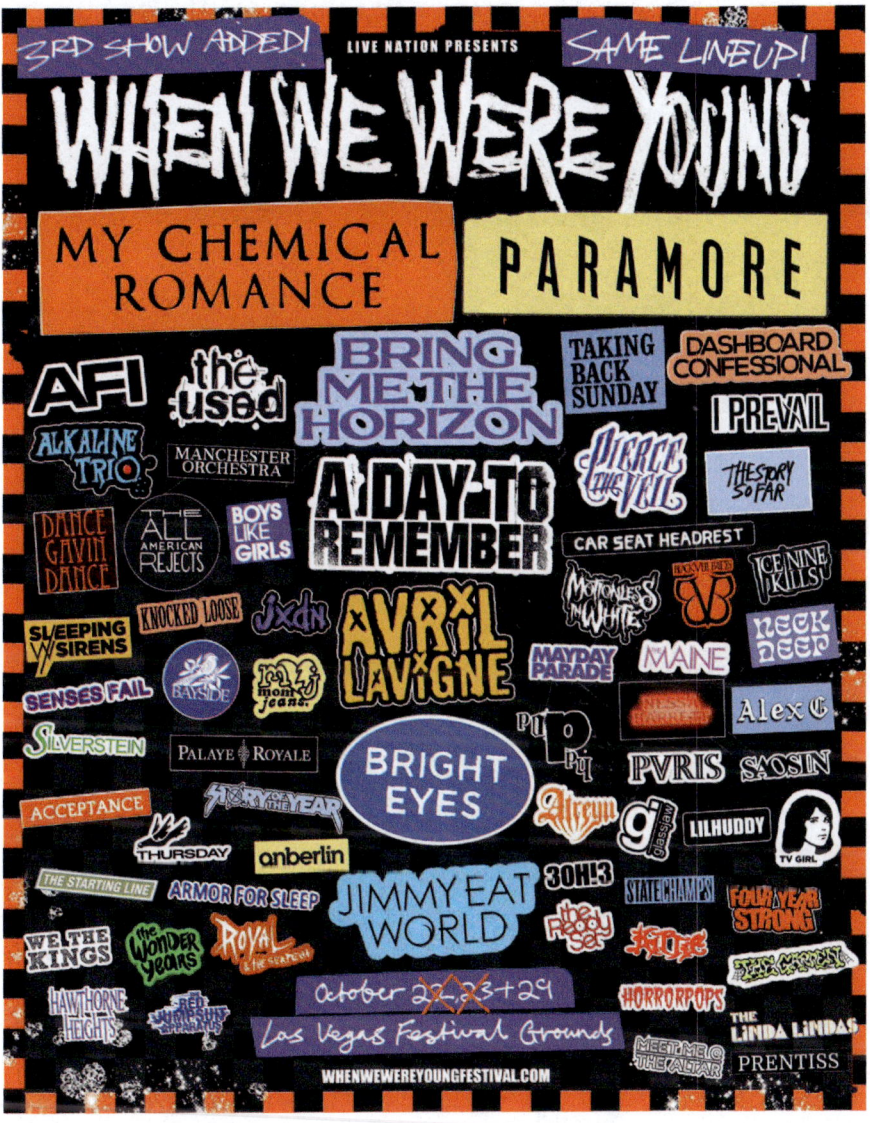

The Fans Have Their Say #15 My Chemical Romance

The Fans Have Their Say #15 My Chemical Romance

And another one that was rebooked…

Printed in Great Britain
by Amazon